My Mother's
SUITCASE

My Mother's
SUITCASE

Wanda Lynn Lefler

Charleston, SC
www.PalmettoPublishing.com

My Mother's Suitcase

Copyright © 2022 by Wanda Lynn Lefler

All rights reserved.

First Edition

Hardcover ISBN: 978-1-63837-178-6
Paperback ISBN: 978-1-63837-179-3
eBook ISBN: 978-1-63837-180-9

This work depicts actual events in the life of the author's family as truthfully as recollection permits. While all persons within are actual individuals, some names and identifying characteristics have been changed to respect their privacy.

Prologue

A Place to Store Your
Treasures and Troubles

We take our belongings here and there. We do so in all kinds of bags. The duffle bags are not new forms of baggage, ask the military. Their shapes have been changed somewhat and they are covered with advertisements, available in many colors, made with numerous types of materials and used by all ages. They are often seen slung over shoulders of athletes including those participating in the Olympics.

The bags on wheels with many zippered compartments are commonplace, whether for a trip out of the country or a sleepover down the street. All types of bags are used as carry-ons to cram in the overhead compartments on planes or in the back of an SUV.

The hard-shell luggage comes in a variety of colors which helps you notice it on the conveyor belts at the airport. This model probably is the one that most resembles the suitcases of decades ago (with the exception of attached wheels).

Throughout the years there have been other suitcases, bags, even decorated pillowcases, to tote our belongings from one point to another. My mother however, always had luggage. When one piece no longer was needed because it did not match a new set, it was given a different job and its placement changed, often to the closet instead of an attic. In many ways you may think it received a promotion in the world of luggage. My mother taught me the value of a suitcase and its contents.

***

Family Ranking

Family is supposed to be our safe place
Very often, it is the place where we find the deepest heartache.
—IYANLA VANZANT, IYANLA VANZANT QUOTES

I am sharing the story of part of my life. Yes, it is one of the more challenging times like a lowcountry hurricane descending upon the unprepared, sweeping those away from their homes with strong winds and flood waters. This is the story of members of my family. It is based on true events, some which are downright ugly (the ones we never talk about and pretend did not happen, not in our family). My mother wrote down the secrets kept in our family and locked them in a small green suitcase—the size of luggage used for overnight stays.

Family members are made of bits and pieces picked up here and there. Some show cracks, others just normal wear and tear. Each family has their own system of ranking order. Some members catch on quickly learning how to program it all to function on their behalf.. Others may eventually notice and then verbalize their displeasure about their place in the lineup claiming, "It's not fair." They fall victim to the game either by choice or fear. Some spend a lifetime keeping up with the ranking order and voice their opinion frequently to anyone that will listen. Occasionally, the favored may turn out in the end of it all to be favored the least due to circumstances. Others do not pay attention to the system and the whole nonsense of listing favorites. There is not a lot of support of one another in the type of families, when someone is keeping score.

WANDA LYNN LEFLER

I once read about a theory that we (you and I), often create a family to work out the problems from our own original family. I have often tossed it up in my head like bopping a brightly colored balloon from side to side. Sometimes I think "There is a lot of truth in the theory." Other times I think, "Who would invite a south wind blowing 140 miles an hour to slam through them again?"

There is a tremendous amount of consideration to unravel the chaos of family dynamics. Perhaps we do this attempt at righting the past without realizing it. If the theory were to be applied, I would marry and create a family with my partner much like the family I started with in life. The one I marry, would be attempting to satisfy his/her unfinished business from his/her family of origin. It does not sound like a fun party game to me.

My family of origin were known as the Leflers. I was the first-born child of Bobby and Inga Lefler. If I enacted the scenario with the Lefler unit, which character do I play to repair the cracks from my childhood?

Am I to be my mother, Inga (a Norwegian woman who left home at age fifteen, lying not only about her age but also about whether she could swim so she could be hired on a Norwegian cruise ship)? Pretty sure she left with what she was wearing, and a few toiletries shoved into a woolen drawstring bag. Traveling all around the world before most graduate from high school. She was escaping choices others made for her future.

Would I somehow choose someone to fill the role as my husband to serve, in my daddy, (Bobby's) place? I bet Bobby left with what little belongings he had in a "poke" (as my Great Aunt Inez would call a paper grocery bag). He left to become a career sailor in the U.S. Navy at age seventeen, to slide pass a possible lifetime working in a southern cotton mill. No, he was not cut out to be a millworker. I heard him say, "No siree, I did not want to be called a 'lint head.'" Lint head was a slang term referring to the cotton mill workers because after a shift exiting the mill with cotton lint could be seen stuck in their hair.

That was not for him. He became a man of his own, exceling and climbing in rank in the military. Once he became a family man, he had other hobbies he utilized or they could be considered tactics to keep him busy and away like fishing and tinkering with race car engines. Distant emotionally and in body as much as possible, there was an invisible sign around him that said, "Children are to be seen not heard." Flashing in neon, "Do not look my way for anything." It reminded me of old clips of the actor W.C. Fields when he would say, "Get away from me kid. You're bothering me."

BOBBY FISHING

In this theoretical family, one of my children would need to be incredibly bright, beautiful and play a stringed instrument, — A fearless and bold child. taking any challenge head on like my sister Selma. A young girl that rode on the school bus with her described seeing Selma for the first time, "When she walked on the bus with her hair styled in a shag, city clothes and those platform shoes, everyone went quiet, and all eyes were on her. It was the most beautiful thing I had ever seen up to that point in my life. I wanted to be just like her."

SELMA AND WANDA
RIGHT TO LEFT

Perhaps my eldest child will be more like myself, always busy with some project, drawing or sewing, a bit scared of everything, even spelling tests. Yet I pushed through, not realizing that not all people felt fear when the teacher announced, "Take out a plain piece of paper. It is time for a spelling test," My heart would pound so hard I could feel the pulsating in my ears. It was as if someone was standing next to me and pounding on a wooden door with a walking stick demanding to be let in.

I had studied the words, knew the correct spelling for the words and usually scored one hundred percent. Despite studying, nausea washed over me even before I knew what nausea was. It felt as though at any moment, a huge wave would crash above my head and the under tow would drag me to the bottom of the sea.

The only thing to calm the jitters was to be prepared with practice tests and making word flashcards. Preparation helped in giving me something to do, like swimming out to meet the large wave that has yet crested. If anyone noticed how scared I was of drowning, *somewhat similar to failing*, they did not throw out a life ring. And I did not spot a lifeguard anywhere.

Although two big girls in my sixth- grade class, must have viewed me as their lifeguard. Together threatening to beat me up after school if I did not let them see my paper during the spelling test. They were bigger, more the size of grown women with rounded hips. It was an on-going challenge to keep their hip huggers from sliding down so far that the crack of their fanny was in view. Those girls were yanking their pants up and their shirts down all day to keep their bellies or fannies from showing. It is no wonder they did not have time to study the spelling words.

The spelling test was enough but taking the risk to cheat would have had made my heart pound at a rate causing lightheadedness. A high risk for me to be flat on the floor like the ocean had spit me out onto the sand. Lucky for me the teacher was on watch. She walked around the room calling out the spelling words, up and down each aisle slowly. Her head turning like an owl's so she did not miss a thing. The girls did not blame or beat me up because they could not pirate anyone's paper. The teacher rescued me and did not know it.

The anxiety for success of academic achievement was high. I wanted my parents to be proud of me, at least equally so as they were my sister. She did not study and brought home report card perfection every time, all A's with glowing remarks from her teachers,

The pressure may have come from the fact that neither parent had graduated high school and like all parents they wanted better for their girls. Certainly, better than running to escape plans others had concocted for them.

It may be that we all are dragging the baggage from our family of origin— The hurt and disappointment of expectations too high for anyone to achieve is hard to leave behind. No one told us we would need things like forgiveness, tolerance, and trust packed among our things for life. Nope, our suitcases were packed for us by others.

How hopeless is it for those of the families from generations of failed marriages, family secrets built of broken trusts and not feeling good enough?

It leads to mental health issues such as anxiety, and depression going unchecked for generations. It is a great breeding ground for developing unhealthy relationships. Consider the consequences to the creating of a new family if both members of the bridal party come from such challenged beginnings.

***

NIELSON HOME SNUBBA, NORWAY

Black Boots
Marching — Norway 1940

A lot that weighs you down isn't yours to carry
—SHANNON MERRETT, TRUE WORDS OF LIFE 2020

The German occupation of Norway brought Hitler's elite soldiers marching into the village where my mother was born, Snubba, (a village twenty-two to twenty-three miles northwest of the city of Narvik). Narvik was a huge supplier of iron ore. Hitler wanted to lay claim on it.

Inga's father, Nils was an architect's assistant so the house may have benefitted from his skills when it was being constructed. Not such a benefit when chosen as the place the soldiers would set up and reside while in the area.

Nikolai "Nils" Nielsen was gone away from home as part of the Norwegian resistance, leaving his wife with a newborn son and a young daughter, Inga. All in the village had heard the rumors that the SS soldiers were to come through their village. A day when many German planes had flown over low, rattling the windows put those in Snubba on notice and on edge. Many had left the village. Other neighbors were frightened to show themselves outside their homes.

When darkness fell the sound of possibly drums could be heard in the distance. As the sound drew closer it was clear, it was not the beating of drums but the stomping of soldiers coming closer to their homes, their village, their Norway. The men left in the village were older. The guns were gone with the younger men off fighting with the resistance and they were not there to offer any resistance to this sound of an army marching toward them. Some neighbors turned out all lights barely breathing so as not to make a sound—anything not to be noticed by the soldiers with the tall black boots marching in unison down the village's main road. Neighbors brave enough, peaked out from the edge of the curtains only after the thundering sound of boots pounding the village's iced dirt road had passed their home. The heartbeats of all within an earshot beat faster as the intended stomps of intimidation neared their home.

The hope of those that stayed in Snubba, a small village nestled midway of a mountain, that the Germans would not have a need for it and march on. The villagers did not know it had been deemed the place to run the communication lines for the operation in nearby Narvik. The lines would go up the mountain, the village was nicely planted near. The soldiers was to set up in the village for the duration.

The black boots came to a sudden halt. Someone was shouting German words not understood by the little girl hiding in what was the chosen house. Inga leaned over, whispering to her mother as they huddled on the floor in the closet under the stairs. The broom and mop hung on the inside of the door. The smell of the harsh soap in the bucket near Inga's little feet made her eyes and nose itch. Her mother, breathing heavily, tried not to cry from fright because her little girl would then cry too. She held Inga's tiny little head close to hers while praying to God and the old Norse Gods for this child to be still and quiet as her baby boy tightly bundled slept in the crook of her other arm.

The smell of smoke pervaded the room—the fire doused only minutes before the soldiers had entered the village. She thought of how she would need to scrub the soot from the white walls although that was quickly replaced by other thoughts. Oh, how she wished those boots would start marching further down the village road and beyond the mountain.

The soldiers did not knock at the door of the chosen house. They did not pound on the door and wait for someone to come and answer it. One of the black boots with one kick knocked open the locked door. It broke the chair placed under the doorknob meant to hold them out. Inga yelped and jumped during the commotion. Selma Andrea tightened her grip on Inga, leaning her head in, and oh so quietly whispering in her ear "Shhhhhh." Worry beset her. Her stomach tightened at the very thought that either child may give away their hiding place.

The first big boot through the door stood aside as another larger shadowed figure in black boots stepped into their home, listening, and scanning the room in skilled precision for the source of the yelping. The silence was as loud as the planes the Germans had flown over the house earlier in the day.

The screaming in Selma Andrea's ears was the pounding of her own heart pulsing in her head. More black boots stomping against the wooden floor joined the towering figure. No word was spoken. The looming tall, dark figure directing by pointing to different corners in the space, then a match was struck, and a candle was lit. The boots no longer stomping together seemed to be shuffling all around them like vultures ready to pick apart a carcass. Each step came closer to the only safety the young mother had carved out for herself and her two little ones. The boots had come to a stop right outside the makeshift door, as did the woman's breathing. Hands sliding across the wall is all that could be heard as the other boots had quieted. A yank on the boarded door caused light to spill into the closet betraying the created space of refuge.

A man in black boots bent down with his gun, smiling, as his eyes met the dark brown eyes of the mother. He motioned with the gun for her to climb out of the den she created, to the room where they once had gathered as a family; the room where the little girl played as the mother went about her daily chores, where they talked about the day's events and sometimes would sing and dance. The room that was now filled with large men with their pants stuffed into large black boots. Inga, not comprehending the danger, was the first one to climb out and pop right up on her socked feet. Her eyes went from the floor almost to the ceiling of the room, looking at what seemed like the giant trolls in the stories her mother had told her. She ran to grab on to her mother's dress, trying to climb under the skirt to hide. Her mother stood quiet and still. Inga could see one of the trolls had his hand wrapped around the back of her mother's neck like a wicked vine.

Selma Andrea seemed so small standing next to the evil troll in black boots. She was such a contrast with her reddish-brown hair and creamy white skin. Her ample breasts—due to her breastfeeding—were barely noticed because of the long-sleeved blouse wrapped by a skirt at the waist and draped over by an apron. If the baby were not in her arms, no one would have noticed she had delivered three weeks ago due to all the layers of clothing. She seemed so small in her stocking feet standing among the soldiers in black boots. The largest man dressed all in black appeared to be in charge because when he spoke, all the other black boots stood at attention and snapped to his words. He nodded at two of the others. The black boots that had kicked in the farmhouse's door scooped up Inga and another nearby snatched the infant from Selma Andrea's arms. Inga screamed her hands tightly wrapped in her mother's skirt.

The black boots angrily speaking to the screaming girl pried her hands away from her mother. The girl's screams became piercing, the soldier reacted by placing one of his large, rough hands over her mouth. Inga did stop the annoying siren sound because his hand smelled like something her dad used to start a fire outside. This thick calloused hand covered both her nose and mouth making it difficult to breathe. She kicked her legs and swung her arms wildly and yet he still held her. The door to the house was slammed shut. Inga, with the last bit of fire in her, clamped her teeth into the palm of Mr. Black Boots. Now he was the one yelping as he slung the child to the ground. The boots started toward her only to be met by the pair of boots holding her baby brother. Those boots slid closer to Inga, lying in the icy snow still and quiet. The black boots with rough smelly hands yelled at the other soldier. Again, the soldier slid his boots to block access to the motionless child. This soldier was much quieter when he spoke. The few words he spoke had the others moving back toward the door of the house.

The little girl, with hair darker than her mother's, was shaking. She was not wearing a sweater or coat nor shoes on her feet. No way could she last long in the frigid Norwegian winter. The soldier with the infant in his arm thought it may be a kinder act to leave her there to drift away. Perhaps lay the baby beside her and walk away. The activity in the house would quite possibly make them orphans. This soldier thought of his daughter, around the same age as the child in the snow. He would come to the girl's defense many times during the occupation of the farm.

SELMA ANDREA ON HER WEDDING DAY LATE 1930'S

Selma Andrea lifted her head and looked the large German intruder in the eyes. She did not blink. He smiled as he took her blank stare as surrendering. He moved his hand behind her, untying the apron. The woman affixed her eyes to the corner of a darkened windowpane. She thought about a small nick caused by one of Nil's shoes flying off as they danced with their daughter. Then they all laughed. She had asked Nils to fix the nick so it would not become a crack that could shatter the glass. Odd how her perspective had changed, for now she filled all her focus in the nick to transport her to those happier days.

Suddenly the woman was lifted and pushed face down unto the wooden table, her legs dangling, her feet unable to touch the floor. Her long skirt was lifted over her head as someone grabbed her hands and skirt from the other side of the table. She lost her view of the corner of the window, so she closed her eyes— not tightly— ever so easily. She could feel as her underwear was yanked down and left to rest on one of her feet. It was a conscious decision she made to not tighten her muscles, not her hands, wrists, or legs. She did not tighten her bottom, although it was still bleeding from the birth of her son and no tightening of her knees or feet. She was not going to kick. She would not resist. How could she? They were going to do with her what they will. If she did not fight, maybe she could live through this to see her children. They needed someone to care for them. It had to be her because there was no one else. If it were not for her children, she would fight like a Viking shield maiden of the old times. The intruders would have had to slit her throat and kill her to gain what they were lusting after. Her eyes filled with hot, salty tears. They stung the corner of her eyes as they exited, puddling at her cheek which was pressed against the table. She thought her eyes were betraying her. "I cannot feel this. I must not feel this." Her body wanted her to scream and plead for the intruders to *stop* as they each took turns shoving themselves into her tender body. Blood ran down her legs as hot as the tears that had puddled onto the table. Selma Andrea did not yelp or cry out for help. Somehow, she drifted off, thinking of the stories her mother once told her of the warrior women fighting alongside the men in the wars during the time of The Vikings.

An excruciating pain shook the battered woman from her deep state of numbness. Although she attempted to leave the waking state and return to the numbness, the pain would not allow her. Straw poked through her clothing scratching her neck and her back, but it was a mild annoyance compared to the entirety of her body. Movement would surely cause more pain. Reasoning if she were dead, she would not feel pain and if that was true, would it not have been best to have died? The horrid smell overcame the thoughts. It was not any smell she had smelled before. Where was it coming from? Perhaps she had died, and she was adrift somewhere between heaven and hell. God may not allow her into heaven because she did not fight back and allowed the intruders to enter her being. "Oh, My Heavenly Father, I did not allow them to steal my soul. Please forgive me. I did not fight back, so that I may protect my babies," she silently mouthed her prayer.

Her eyes snapped open searching her surroundings. The hayloft with the ladder leaning against it, was directly above her. She noted the few farm animals in their stalls. There was a blanket covering a lump close to one of the sheep and she recognized a blanket by her side as the one knitted by her dearest cousin Unni, for Oskar. Selma Andrea denied the pain and turned toward the bundle. Her breasts were leaking and aching, for it had been more hours than she could imagine since he suckled. The young mother loosened her blouse, leaned up balanced on her right elbow to ready herself to feed her darling son.

Unwrapping the blanket to allow him to cradle himself against her bare skin but wondered why the infant did not move. "He is still sleeping," she thought as she continued to open the blanket noticing the diaper had filled and seeped through his gown. The liquid waste was on the socks she had made for him, (blue with a ribbon running through stitches at the top to tie and keep them on his tiny feet). Lifting the gown, she observed that his legs and feet still had not moved. The mother sickened to question, was the cold from her hands or were his little legs cold? Dread came to visit, sitting on Andrea's heart. The mom could not lift her eyes to the babe's face to confirm what she knew to her core. How could she endure so much and lose—lose her baby? With a blank stare on her face a cold strike of despair ran through her abused body. She whispered softly, "Oskar, come on now, wake up for mommy." She picked him up and pressed his face with her breast while stroking his face, hoping he would open his mouth like a little bird and latch on. Oskar did not latch on. His tiny face was cold and pale and his lips, like his fingertips, tinged blue.

Another cold strike ran through her body hitting her chest as if her heart had frozen and stopped. She wrapped her newborn back in his blanket and laid him in the straw. Somehow, she managed to push against one of the stalls to help her stand. Pain radiating from where the babe had entered the world just three weeks ago did not matter. The numbness settled in. It was silent in this numbness. No tears or agonizing screams, just a shuffling of her feet out the barn door to the cold. She recognized the earlier smell. It was not her dead baby. The putrid smell was from her. Her blood mixed with the intruder's deposits in her body now dried against her soft skin. It was too much for her to take in. Selma Andrea bent over and heaved up what little contents she had in her into the freshly fallen snow. A large clot of blood released itself, slid down her leg, darkening the snow a deep dark red. The young woman that had vowed not to fight back to protect her children, fell to her knees and collapsed into the snow.

The woman with a tiny girl and an infant boy was tossed out of her home and told that if they wanted shelter, they could go to the barn. The soldiers helped themselves to everything the farm had to offer; all the food that had been harvested and preserved for the winter, the farm animals slaughtered, (not caring if some were pets and had been given names by the little girl living at the farm). The firewood that had been cut, chopped, and stacked was tossed in, log after log, to keep the SS warm while sleeping in another man's bed.

***

NIKOLAI NIELSEN

Risk Drowning.....if You Stay on Land

Inga's mother died several years after the war ended. Inga was fifteen years old at the time and she was left to live with her father and his girlfriend. The same girlfriend that Nils would allow Inga to come along to visit while her mother was sick. Inga felt torn between going with her adulterous father or staying to care for her ill mother. Nils always convinced his daughter that her mother was a strong woman, she would be all right and they would be back soon.

Inga tagged along as he went to sweet talk and sometimes go into the barn with Atla, (his side woman) for what seemed like a very long time. She knew what he was doing when he came out of the barn zipping up his pants. The woman came out rushing right after him pushing her skirts in place with straw clinging to her sweater and her hair. Tried as she might, there was no mistaking what they were doing in the barn, and it was not feeding the goats.

Inga knew her mother had cancer. Selma Andrea had no control if she would live or die, not unlike when the soldiers came. She had no control if they were going to rape her or not and they did. She was a woman who wished she had died a lifetime ago during the war—she prayed to God to let her die —to take her as her son was taken. Yet, she survived and for what? She wished every day that she was dead. She certainly felt dead inside. Selma Andrea had even tried to slow her heart to make it stop beating, so she would not feel the pain she had for not protecting her children from the evils of war.

She long ago had stopped reaching out to hold her daughter. She did not want her to feel the frailty she herself cursed. Her husband had returned from war and wanted to know where his son, Oskar was (wanting to see what a big boy he had become). All she could do was take him to his grave. Nils was angry at his wife for not protecting their son. "You should have protected him with your own life. If he is dead, you should be dead," he said, standing at the infant's gravesite marked only by a small stone.

Nils was so angry that he did not bed down again with his wife. He took up with another woman from a nearby village. The worst part of it all is that he would take their daughter with him when he went to be with his lover. She never discussed it with her daughter because she knew she was dying and had no answers for her.

She was a bit relieved Nils never wanted to lay with her because the soldiers had caused terrible destruction to her vagina and rectal area so that it would be incredibly painful. It was not odd that this was the region of her body that had cancer. The area she had delivered both her daughter and son, once giving life, was taking what life she had left.

The doctor told her the soldiers carried many sexual diseases from their escapades. The damage they had done to her was what caused her disease and years of urinary and bowel problems. If she had seen the doctor sooner it would not have prevented her problems, only prolonged them. Selma Andrea had made peace with herself in those regards. She was ready to die. Many regrets but none greater than letting go of her daughter so soon. She prayed and wept every day that God would take care of Inga.

*＊＊

The day her mother died, Inga still felt abandoned and so very much alone in the world. She was also very angry at her mother for leaving her behind just as she did not protect Oskar when the soldiers marched to their house. Angry, because she watched her mother wither away only crying and saying prayers. Prayers did not keep her alive or make her well. Her prayers did not keep them safe from the Germans. Her prayers were as futile as her mother's advice to not beg for food from the Germans. If Inga had not gotten food from the Germans by jumping around like a dog or kangaroo, she would have died like Oskar.

Oskar that froze to death when her mother wore a sweater that could have warmed him. Oskar that was dressed in her christening gown, wrapped tightly in a blanket, and placed on top of boxes in the tool shed because they had to wait for the ground to thaw before they buried him. Inga saw him stacked up in the window for weeks. She would run fast hoping what took him did not take her. All the while her mother prayed. Her prayers did not keep Oskar warm.

What good are her prayers? She is dead.

Nils had Atla move in the day they buried Selma Andrea. Inga mounted a protest but was quickly reminded in whose house she resided. Nils soon went to bed, the one he shared with Inga's mother now replaced by the Atla woman. He was too drunk to put on a show and fell off to sleep. Nils awoke the next morning, made himself presentable, and headed off to work.

✳✳✳

The woman slept late, evidently not concerned with chores to be done on a farm. She finally, awoke only when her sister (Heidrun) showed up at the house. The sister had much darker features than Atla, the fair skin often accompanying red hair.

Atla being the younger of the two sisters was not a small woman, yet she was smaller than her sister. Knocking on the door with her walking stick, when no one answered Heidrun did not hesitate, she pushed the door open and waltzed right on in like she belonged there. The older sister bellowed the younger sister's name a few times. Inga watched from a crack in the door in an upstairs room. Heidrun started looking around as if she knew no one was eyeing her movements. First, she looked in the pantry mumbling some kind of comment as she slammed it closed. Opening and shutting cabinets as if taking inventory, again, she yelled her sister's name just as the woman taking the place of Inga's mother came shuffling out of the bedroom downstairs. She was wearing Selma Andrea's robe!

Inga felt hot from head to toe. Her instinct was to run down the stairs and yank the robe off that slutty woman's body. "How dare she! My mother worked for everything, everything! This person comes in and just takes what she wants. All she did was lie down and open her legs," Inga slung open the door and yelled louder than the older sister had bellowed, "Take it off!"

The sisters, startled at the audacity of this child to yell in their direction, each turned and looked at her with expressions not of pity for one that had viewed her mother lowered in the ground less than two days prior. The round faces held grimaced lines formed tightly around their downward facing mouths— a look of no tolerance for this screaming, motherless child.

Inga, noting the formidable pair straightened her spine, tilted her head up, placed her hands on her hips with feet spaced evenly with her shoulders, and stomped her left foot to emphasize her demand, "Take off my mother's robe! Now!"

The women roared in laughter. Atla, the sister in the robe, started to dance around sashaying the bottom of the robe side to side as if she were a dancer at a French saloon. Infuriated, Inga barreled down the steps, collided with all her might (as much might as a ninety-two pound girl could muster), into the dance hall mimic, sliding into chairs, knocking them both over. One of the chair's heavy wooden legs hit Inga's head.

Inga, dazed, lay still on the floor, not moving the chair that had landed on top of her small body, her eyes closed. She felt above her right eyebrow, as all the heat she had while standing on the landing above now seeped from her and dripped to her earlobe before hitting the wood floor without a sound. It crossed her mind that she may be dead until she heard Heidrun laughing. Atla yelled as she kicked the head of the girl sprawled on the floor. Inga yelped as she opened her eyes, wrapping her head with her arms, monitoring if another kick was coming her way.

Heidrun grabbed her sister, whispering something to her. The girl, stunned, with both sides of her head pounding like a snare drum in a parade, was relieved as Atla was distracted. Lifting the heavy chair across her chest and abdomen proved not a possibility so she slid it across her body until she was no longer imprisoned. Inga was trying very hard to not call attention to herself with hopes of getting out of the house before the sisters could do more harm to her. Now freed, she snapped up on her feet despite a bleeding, banging head. She flew toward the door, flung it open and headed out. Heidrun screamed, "Hey, where is she going?" Atla hurried to the door but by the time she looked out, Inga had vanished. She slammed the door shut and said, "She will be back. She has nowhere else to go."

Inga's feet were clad only in socks. It was cold with snow on the ground. Her feet were stinging. Not wanting to make it easy if the sisters were inclined to hunt her down, she had run toward the woods then doubled back to behind the barn. She watched where she was placing her feet (it was a barn with cows and a horse). Noting she had lost one of her socks during her wild dash. She climbed up to the loft where she had created her own place with a pillow, a blanket, extra clothes and books in a far back corner. This was a place to find respite when her dad was throwing back drinks. He was mean when he became inebriated. It was best to clear out.

This is the place the girl came to when her mother had died. She cried as she recalled all the tough times her mother had gotten through before succumbing to cancer. It was horrible to watch how her mother struggled with an illness and continued to work the farm, kept the house clean, and cooked—always cooking. A month before she passed from this earth, she no longer could do those things. Inga had always helped her mother with chores. When Selma Andrea struggled to get out of bed, it was her daughter that took over. Nils would have grumbled should food not be on the table when he walked in the door, cancer or not. This space in the corner of the loft held a whole lot of painful memories. It was ironic for it to be the girl's safe haven.

About an hour after she left fleeing from the house, Inga saw the nasty sisters leave. They were most likely headed to town for shopping of some sort. Inga decided she would climb down to go back in the house so she could clean up. She really needed to look at her head and tend to it. All she knew was that the bleeding had clotted but the pounding continued on both sides of her head.

Opening the barn door ever so slowly just in case the sisters decided to return, she poked her badgered head out first to investigate the surrounding area. She saw tracks heading away from the house (hers and then the sisters). No tracks going toward the house so she decided it may be best to go out the back and track footsteps toward the woods, go through the woods to the back door and up the stairs to her room.

It was mid-afternoon when the door opened and closed. Inga assumed the dastardly sisters were back from shopping. She heard a deep man's voice—and it was not her dad's voice. He laughed loud and heartily, a sound that sent an eerie chill up the girl's spine. The women's voices were cackling like two old crones to Inga's ear.

Footsteps coming up the stairs were the familiar ones of Atla, her dad's sleeping buddy. The woman opened the door to the girl's room—no knock tells of the lack of boundaries or manners (probably both), the girl thought. The woman was smiling when making eye contact. "Uh oh, something is not right. The she-ogre never smiles at me," passed through Inga's mind.

Atla started to speak. She and Heidrun had devised a plan to redecorate the house so she could make it hers and not her mother's house. The only problem was that it took money. The plan included Inga having to work for the needed funds. It would teach her humility and to "not dare ever do what she had done this morning." Inga stood still, not inquiring, not curious for her dad would take care of this woman when he arrived home in a few hours.

Atla smirked and went on despite the girl's silence. Heidrun had the idea of bringing a friend for Inga to meet. She asked as if a second idea had popped in her mind, "You are a virgin aren't you princess?" Still no verbal response, but Inga's gaze became fierce as if she was trying to incinerate the despicable woman's brain into ashes. Atla, a bit unsettled, carried on with the plan concocted. "You see the man friend of Heidrun's waiting downstairs is going to come in your room to teach you about the work you will be doing. He will be coming to visit you every day until we are sure you will be ready to make a lot of money. The money will be Heidrun's and mine, not yours. If you tell your father, then you will soon be lying beside your mother. Do you understand me? I will be in charge of you—of where you go, what you do, who you see and who you fuck! You can wear the damn robe of your mother's as long as you take it off when you lie down. You are going to be a whore for me."

Atla (the want-to-be madame), called out a man's name. Inga heard the louder footsteps ascending the steps. The girl rushed across the room toward Atla, who quickly exited the room. Inga grabbed the doorknob, yanking it, but could not open the door. A knock accompanied by a mumbling of the man's voice and the howling laughter of the wicked woman going down the stairs had Inga considering climbing out the window and jump from the roof.

She moved from the door to lunge toward the window, just as the man opened the door. This man was huge! He had to bend his head down to enter her room. Inga could not open the window, so she darted toward the door. The man had sat on the tiny bed. His arm reached out, grabbing the girl, and pulling her to him. The petite fifteen -year-old started to hit the man with her fists clenched tightly, kicking, banging her head against the man's expansive chest—not helping given her earlier injuries to her head. She reached down with her mouth open, not finding a place to bite due to the thick coat. The frightened girl started to scream, and the man clamped his hand over her mouth and whispered in her ear, "Hush," to quiet the girl. She did not let up, violently swinging her arms and legs.

The man stood up holding the girl in one arm as he took off his coat, the other arm switching the hold on the girl. He unzipped his pants, shaking them to the floor by kicking his legs. This move had Inga's mouth uncovered and she screamed at the man, at Heidrun and the loudest threats were for Atla.

The man was shaking the girl to have her hush as he was attempting to free himself from his pants which were still wrapped around his ankles. Her threats did not produce any results. She was frightened more than she had ever been, even more than she was of the Nazi's. She was afraid they would kill her. What this man had on his mind—she was scared she might survive.

The huge tree-like man still had his boots on, struggling to have his pants to go over them. Noticing this, the girl held her mouth open as wide as she could and sunk her teeth into his white belly. The lug head was now the one doing the screaming. He dropped her as he moved his arm to grab the toothed attachment. Inga let go of her bite, falling to the floor and facing the door. Taking advantage of the man cussing as he was assessing his wound, she scooted on all fours to the door, shot up on her feet, unlocked and flung the door open. The man had turned around and fallen to the floor because his pants still had him trapped.

Inga flew down the steps, exiting to the left side of the third step to avoid the women waiting for her at the landing. She went out the door and slammed it behind her. Taking the same route that she had earlier in the day, she rushed into the loft and grabbed all her clothes. stuffing them into a pillowcase. She put on her socks and boots along with a Norwegian sweater and gloves made by her mother. The toboggan hat she pulled on over her head was a gift from her mom as well. Inga knew the sisters may have been too uninspired to search for her in the morning, but things had changed, and they would be hunting her like she was a lost diamond ring. The man may want to teach her a lesson or worse, for getting away while leaving a mark.

* * *

Startled, she burrowed into the straw in the far corner of the loft when she heard the women enter the barn squabbling over blame of how the plan all went wrong. Her limbs were trembling. She pressed her lips together hard to slow the fast pace of her breathing, concerned it would alert the sisters to her location.

Inga noticed an altered taste in her mouth. Quickly identifying it as the huge man's blood, she fought the urge to spit it out (that would alert the wicked pair below). Instead of spitting, she allowed her saliva to pool in her left cheek and to drain out into the hay. She wiped her tongue on the lower part of her sleeve. The sudden hygiene problem, as awful as it was, had distracted her from the evil lurking below.

After the sisters agreed it was the fault of the man for not handling the girl as planned, they exited the barn the same way they entered. Inga decided to wait for a short while. She gathered what she could carry, all the while thinking she sure wished she had made better plans. The girl knew there was no way to re-enter the house to get some of her things. She had no idea her dad would move Atla in the house so soon after her mother had died.

Shaking the "coulda, woulda, shoulda" thoughts out of her brain, she knew there were other things to be done.

* * *

Escape by Sea

Inga's neighbor from three houses down in the village was so very helpful when her mother was ill. The woman (by the name of Agot) had told Inga before and after her mother's passing that if there was a time when she could help her to just ask. Agot had watched how Nils would leave when his wife was very much in need of help. She also knew the what, the where and the who he was more willing to offer his time. Inga heard her tell her mother it was shameful, but she need not worry she and others were there to help.

Inga had left the barn and the only home she had ever known and was knocking on the door hoping Agot would follow through with her offer to help. Berrent, (the husband of dear Agot) opened the door to see the dark eyed girl looking so lost standing in front of him. He had her come in and sit in a chair near the fire. His eyes caught his wife's as she rushed to the girl. Agot placed her arms around her, and the girl released all the tension she had felt. Incoherent at times, Agot decided to warm, feed, and have the girl rest before going on with this story.

***

Agot showed her to the guest bed. Inga slumped down and fell into a deep sleep. Agot in her fairy Godmother role, removed her heavy sweater, gloves and hat. Her shoes were already drying by the fireplace. A heavy quilt was placed over this skin-and-bones girl. Like so many others in the country, she had gone through far more in her short lifetime than most in a very long-lived life. Agot stroked this woman-child's hair off her face. "Such a tired little face," thought the woman. She prayed for her neighbor to have much peace in her life.

Inga did not wake until the next morning. Agot was standing at the sink. Noticing the presence of her guest she asked if she drank coffee. Inga nodded her head yes as she looked around the room wrapping her arms around herself. Agot, as if reading her mind, told her they were alone for a while at least. Berrent was out taking care of the animals. Sitting the coffee in front of her guest, Agot pulled a chair out and sat down directly across from her. "So little one, I am glad you showed up at my door last night. I have worried about you. Remember I told you if I could help you, I would do so?" Agot quietly smiled. "Tell me what brings you to our door?"

Inga had tears slowly rolling down her face one side and then the other. No sounds accompanied the tears. She sat quietly for several minutes. As she thought about where to or how to start revealing the events of the day before, her head hurt. Recalling the kick to the head, she reached up lightly placing a finger where the blood had felt warm. It was tender to even a light touch but not bleeding. The girl silently mouthed the words of the past day's events. As she continued, her voice became a bit more audible for the elder's ears to hear.

Agot leaned in closely so as not to miss a word. Her eyes began to sting too. Those 60 plus-old eyes emptied what felt like salty lava on her skin. Tears singed with the pain from deep inside where the hurt is often buried, yet unfortunately not forgotten. This tiny young woman was attesting just one day of such things. Agot knew Inga may never recite these words again.

When all was told that was to be told, the old woman slipped out of her chair to fetch a cloth. She doused it in cold water and patted the young woman's face leaving it with her to hold on her forehead. She eased back in the chair at the table. It was her time to be quiet and to think what to do to help. The girl could not stay here for her father would demand she come home and, given the details of yesterday, that was not an option. She thought of the few relatives she and her husband had left in the world and they were elderly, and some had help coming in to care for them. Agot thought of friends she and Berrent had over the years—someone who may be of assistance popped into her head. It jolted her up out of her seat and she began looking for her coat and such to go to the barn to see her husband.

These sudden movements sent a crease across Inga's face. Agot noticed, patted the younger one on the shoulder telling her not to worry. Adding that she was not going to her father. No indeed, she had an idea that may solve the problem and she had to speak to Berrent to see if it could be accomplished. She assured Inga she would be back. Leaving out the door she said she was "off to the barn" as the cold air pushed itself in as if it needed to go and sit a spell by the fire.

It was all a rush, rush, hurry, hurry after Agot returned from the barn. The woman explained, as they gathered the girl's things up adding a few extra things of Agot's she thought the girl might need. There was a friend that may help. Explaining that it was a woman friend that has been a friend of hers since they were children. They see one another whenever they are able but they write every month.

Berrent had returned from the barn rushing about as if they were late for a very important appointment. He yelled that the truck was ready and waiting. With that as an invitation, Agot shoved a bag in Inga's arms and she snatched up another, pulling the girl along as they bustled toward the door. She looked upon the bewildered girl, taking a nice thick cape with a hood, throwing it over the girl's shoulders, Agot said, "It is not much but it is the best I got and it will keep you warm. Come on now and we will explain on our way."

The couple explained this friend of Agot's never married. No, her dream was to go to sea and the only way she could was to be on one of the Norwegian cruise liners. Mentioning they were the finest ships for the wealthy to travel upon—no doubt about it. The letters they shared told of many wonderful places they visited.

Her friend has worked there for years upon years finally having some top responsibilities. She oversaw the hiring all the staff for the ship's dining, kitchen and cleaning services. The plan was to meet the ship when it comes into port to ask her friend to take Inga on in a position on board. This will give her a means to support herself, so she does not have to return home to face the reality awaiting. Inga nodded, for what other choice did she have?

Agot hoped Inga's age would not be a question, so she told her to say she was eighteen. It still may be a problem because she is so petite. Agot would tell the truth, the girl had been starving during the war. Her mother too was a petite woman and had just died so the girl had wasted to nothing. Another story is that she has no one left in this world, nowhere to live and expressed a deep desire to go to sea knowing that if she were a man she could join the Norwegian Navy, the Merchant Marines or be on a fishing boat. Agot knew her friend would indeed help then.

The time came to meet her friend in two days' time. Berrent stayed at a relative's house when Agot took Inga down to the port. A board had postings of the vessels coming and going. The board indicated the friend's ship had docked as the information said in the last letter Agot had received. Agot led the way to the ship, instructing Inga to wait until she had an opportunity to speak to her friend. Inga did as she was told.

Although Agot had visited many times on the ship, she had always had an invitation to do so. This would be a surprise visit and one asking for a favor. She was apprehensive about how she would be received and if the request would be granted. Her friend was surprised to see her, asking Agot if perhaps she had forgotten that they were to meet. She replied, "No, this was an unexpected visit and I need your help." Concern washed over the friend's face as she rushed to Agot's side asking if she were ill, did she need to sit down or a glass of water? Agot agreed to sit mumbling her health was fine. She asked if her friend had a few minutes to talk to her. Her friend sat while telling Agot, "Well of course and I want to help in any way I can. You are my oldest and dearest friend. I would do anything for you."

The childhood friend listened attentively as the girl's story unraveled on the mostly empty ship. The woman cried as she listened to the horrors of the girl's loss of her mother and the events that transpired soon afterward. Agot was right, the final point to assure Inga a passage on the ship had worked. Agot hugged her friend and promised to write as always. Inga looked relieved and stricken ill at the same time when Agot reached the dock where she had told her to wait. Agot told the child she had gained a position on board. Telling her to take her two bags, report to the dining room, and leave the bags at the door before entering. The tall red-haired woman (her friend Sigrid) was waiting to meet her. Agot grabbed Inga pulling her close to her, hugging her tight. She kissed her on her forehead twice saying, "You are going to be all right, just fine little one. Listen to Sigrid and she will take fine care of you. You write to me and tell me what you are seeing on your travels so this old woman will not worry about you. Sigrid has my address. Save your money. Now, you go on little one and start a new life. Go on with yourself."

Inga promised she would write and managed a, "Thank you for all you and Berrent have done for me. I would have been…" The old woman released her from the embrace, tears wetting them both. Agot turned and walked down the pier. Inga watched as if frozen in a painting. A ship going out blew its horn and snapped Inga back to her current space. She grabbed her bags, taking all the space on the ships ladder going up.

Inga remembered to drop her bags outside the dining room door. Barely able to pull the heavy door open, she managed to enter. She spotted a red-haired woman with her back to her—standing and counting dishes. Inga approached her. Stepping in front of her, she curtsied as her mother had taught her. She stood back up and said, "Miss Sigrid, my good neighbor sent me to see you. I am Inga." The woman had never had anyone curtesy on her behalf and attempted not to laugh. As a smile swept across her face, Sigrid looked over the waif standing in front of her. "You are eighteen?" she inquired. "Just barely ma'am," Inga replied. "And you can swim?" Sigrid zinged an unexpected question. Inga spilled a tale of learning to swim as quickly as she had learned to ski. Her daddy tossed her out of the fishing boat at an early age and she had been swimming ever since. Her fabrication stopped short of swimming with the whales.

Sigrid then called out the name, "Cara, please come here." Immediately, a fair-skinned girl with red curly hair pulled back into a bun at the base of her neck appeared before them. Sigrid ordered as if she was in the military, "Help Inga here with her things. She is to be your new mate, sharing your room and working alongside you in the kitchen. Teach her well and help her obtain the necessary supplies including uniforms. Show her around the ship. Introduce her. And Cara, one last thing. Treat her as you would treat me. Inga is like my family." Cara's eyes peeled wide open, straightening her back she snapped with a resounding, "Yes, of course!"

Inga upgraded from a pillowcase to her first piece of luggage from the ship's store when she received her first paycheck. She was so proud. Inga placed a notebook where she had been writing about the different places she had visited. She slipped a few postcards in between the pages to send to Agot.

* * *

SELMA ANDREA ANDREASSEN (FAR RIGHT) AND FAMILY

INDIGENOUS PEOPLE FROM THE VILLAGE OF LIVANG, NORWAY
IN THE FAR NORTH ABOVE THE ARTIC CIRCLE

Deep Dishes

I Don't Know Where I am Going but I'm on My Way.
—CARL SANDBURG

When I was a girl, much of my mother's story remained not talked about (not that it was being hidden). I did not know to ask her questions for she was mommy. You do not think of your parents having a life when you were not in it. What I did learn of the warrior Inga, was learned first-hand when I was older.

She left Norway at age fifteen to work on a Norwegian cruise ship. First starting in the dining room, clearing the tables of dishes. She told a story once about when the ship had pulled into port. All the staff had to complete their work at their duty stations before disembarking. Everyone was excited and hurried the tasks. Here she was standing in the large dining room with rows of tables filled with dirty dishes. Inga felt her friends would leave her and go ahead onshore without her. As she stood there overwhelmed with the volume of plates, glasses and oh so much silverware, she devised a plan to clean up the dining room in time to join her friends.

Heading to a nearby table, she gathered the ends of the tablecloth, tied them together making it easier to carry. Scurrying like a mouse onto the ship's deck, stopping at corners to check for anyone that may see her, she took a deep breath and heaved the tablecloth with clanking silverware between the rails. Overboard the sack went sailing. One tablecloth bundle after another went to be washed away by the sea or sink to the bottom like a pirate's booty.

This story was fascinating. Inga took a chance of losing her job to take the easy way out. No, she was not caught for her lazy deed. Although there was a considerable delay leaving port because there was no accounting for the missing dishes and silverware.

***

The Chief Ingredients of Bobby

For pride is a spiritual cancer.
it eats up the very possibility of
love or contentment or even common sense
—C.S. Lewis, Mere Christianity

My Great Aunt was the one who told the tales of the family history, including Bobby's youth. She told how he followed his grandfather around like he was stuck like glue to his side. As he became older, he was always messing with that old car of his and tending to that head of hair! Adding, she had told him many a time if he cared as much about his soul as he did about his car and that head of hair, he need not worry about being right with the Lord.

My daddy was an engineer in the sense of engines, preferably motorized ones. The interest took hold during his early years tinkering with automobiles or tractors. If he made them go faster, then all the better. As he grew older, he thrilled in straightening the curves on the rural roads in Cabarrus, North Carolina.

Generations before him found the area good for farming and finding treasure. They were farmers like the grandfather he adored—a grandfather who went out to speak to the highway patrol who had followed Bobby home, right up the driveway with lights flashing. The patrolman was some kind of upset and hot to write a ticket. Luther Shinn was a well-respected man in Cabarrus County. He reasoned with the officer, explaining that young Bobby was on his way to join the navy. The car was going to be parked and covered and it would not be racing around on the road. The officer heeded, not issuing a citation, because the car was not to be back on the road.

Bobby hailed from risk takers as well. John Reed, his four times great grandfather had enlisted as a Hessian soldier then stayed on in the new land of the United States of America to become a farmer in Cabarrus County, North Carolina. It was his son, Conrad who found the first documented commercial gold in the United States on the Reed property one Sunday morning in 1799. The story goes, not knowing what the seventeen-pound yellow rock was, the family used it for a doorstop for a few years. Mr. Reed took it with him on a trip to be identified. Learning it was gold, he sold it for far less than its worth. He would return to the buyer later to obtain more funds to receive the proper amount (closer to the actual value of the "golden doorstop"). This would start the operation of the Reed Gold Mine.

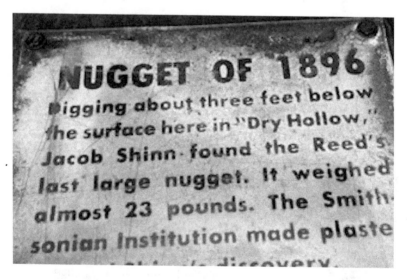

SIGN ONCE POSTED AT REED GOLDMINE, CABARRUS COUNTY, NC

Bobby's great-grandfather, Jacob Shinn a gold miner credited with finding the largest gold nugget from The Reed Gold Mine—a so-called "nugget" at twenty-three pounds. The consequences of gold fever for the Shinn family would cause strife when Jacob's son, Luther Shinn, expressed interest in marrying Flora Irene Furr. Moses Furr, the father of Flora, was a farmer, businessman and postmaster. In the year of 1919, The Charlotte Observer headed his obituary as, "A Prominent Citizen of Cabarrus County, is Dead."

The story was handed down that Mr. Furr did not want his daughter to marry a plain dirt farmer with heritage from the likes of a gold miner. I suppose the way the Shinn's had made their funds to obtain the property was considered less dignified than that of the Furr's (because it was considered quite a gamble or chance to strike for gold).

Eventually, Luther Shinn proved himself worthy and won the hand of Flora Irene Furr, (the only daughter of four that married). Luther Shinn was known throughout his life as a good man. Aunt Inez said of her father, "He never said a cuss word, smoked a cigarette or let alcohol pass his lips." He may have been motivated to prove his worthiness to the Furr family or to live down the risk-taking reputation of his gold mining family. Either way, he set a fine example (possibly one too hard to live up to for his grandson, my father Bobby). Bobby loved and idolized Luther T. Shinn. He was the stable, male figure in Bobby's life due to his parents' divorce.

Yes, Bobby's parents divorced, although it was an uncommon thing to have divorced parents in the 1940's. Bobby, being the oldest, understood when people said crude things about his dad particularly. His dad, (Andrew) earned the nick name that followed him his whole life long, "Preach." He would do exactly as the nick name said, *preach* (the Gospel of Jesus Christ) at the square of the town of Concord (the county seat for Cabarrus County). It was there, in front of the Concord National Bank's double doors, that he stood. His hair was neatly combed, he was dressed in a heavily starched, white, long sleeve shirt with an open bible in his left hand. His dress pants were belted up high on his waist. His best leather oxfords had a different lace in each — one lace had broken, and he did not replace it with a new matching set. He did take the time to shave before he went to where he was called to share the spirit with others. Yelling out scripture to those that passed by. He told them to repent and turn away from their evil ways before it was too late—continuing with the second coming of the Lord was near—all the while giving into his own vice of tasting a nip or more from the flask that had been neatly tucked in his ample, right back pants pocket. The act of tasting was hidden by a large handkerchief that he used to wipe his forehead and mouth.

ANDREW "PREACH" LEFLER

There were times when the police would get a report of a disturbance and sure enough, their ears led them to the square, right in front of the bank. There was Preach standing and attempting to stop people so he could share with them the mighty important good news. The problem was not the message, but the fact that he grabbed people and tried to hold them so they would listen while he spread the message. All this, with alcohol-tinged breath, did not help win over souls. It was putting people off and making them quite uncomfortable.

The business owners were more unhappy and were usually the ones to call for law enforcement. Preach would yell out scripture for all those having transactions at the bank, running errands or shopping in the nearby retail stores.

He was filled with inspiration to summon the folks to give their eternal souls over to their maker or risk an after-life burning in hell. The more insistent his warning became at times—by calling out to certain persons in the area, the more uncomfortable these respectable citizens became as they attempted to enter the bank and the downtown establishments.

The longer it took the police to arrive, the more slurred his speech became. You see, the liquid encouragement spurred on his fervent fire and brimstone warnings to come to Jesus and have their sins washed away clean. Some folks would start to heckle him, questioning his standing with the Lord.

The deputies would arrive and strongly encourage this street preacher to cease and move on. They were often met with resistance along with a proclamation of judgement of the location of their eternal resting place, (not a place with streets of gold and a mansion). The preacher was often handcuffed and given a resting place for the evening.

The incidents, of course were noted in the local paper for all to view. The street preacher's name was noted more than once or twice, and news of the incidents retold. This gives a hint, of why the nickname stuck. It did not help his standing with his former wife's family.

The locals talked and children would pick up the information at the barber shop, gas station or grocery store. Then they were loaded up to come to school poking Bobby, his brother and even their sister with stories of a drunk preacher for a daddy. The shame, although not theirs to carry, was shouldered by Preach's children, (none more so than his eldest son, Bobby). The need to have a fine reputation by hard work and making the right choices, was without a doubt impressed upon the young boy as was the heavy responsibility of picking up the slack due to his father being gone. Bobby's plans to become an outstanding citizen like his grandfather, Luke Shinn, certainly was presented with an obstacle when his father was a frequent mention in the police blotter of the newspaper. Young Bobby's choices in life were greatly influenced by the unsaid rule as to not bring further shame to the family.

Preaching on the streets usually cost the Preach money. He made a living by driving a rig. Andrew usually drove long hauls, placing him out of town and on the road much of the time. When he did come around, his children tried to soak up as much of his attention as possible. Bobby asked where all he had driven that big truck. The boy continued with wanting to know the type of loads he was carrying. He showed so much interest that Andrew told him he would take him with him sometime. The boy immediately wanted to know when. His dad was surprised at actually being taken up on the offer because his eldest son spent most of his free time following his grandfather like he was sewn on to his overalls. Bobby kept tugging on his shirt until Andrew threw out an answer to stop the questions, "Um, it will have to be when you are out of school."

The few visits after this, Bobby was persistent in reminding his dad how many months, then weeks, until school was out. Andrew would shake his head in agreement. He always tried to make these visits as quick as possible (for his pocket was quite a bit lighter when he left). Anytime he drove to the Shinn property, he would be forced to endure an encounter with his wife. She would tell him each time, it was about time he showed his face. Standing with one hand on her hip and her right hand extended, searing him with her deep blue eyes saying, "Well, it is time to pay up. Where's the money preacher man?"

One time, he said under his breath, "I got it you leech," as he reached into his jacket, pulling out a long leather billfold. It did not fold but held the bills flat and straight. Andrew preferred carrying his cash close to his body up front, so it was less likely to be lifted (unlike the back pocket). He had clipped the bills together before he started toward the country so he did not need to waste time counting it out in front of her which he knew would give her a great amount of pleasure. Yes, she would love to watch his stack of bills dwindle, leaving him with little to get by on until his next visit. He thought it was worth it even though he slept in that rig most nights. Andrew was relieved he had not been caught by his boss man when he was sleeping in town on the truck's lot.

Margaret puckered her mouth and produced a kissing sound when Andrew had placed the cash in her hand, quick to tighten her fingers around it, fold it, and place it down the front of her bra. "It is in the bank now. Thank you for the business, make sure your next trip is sooner next time." He stared back at her with his equally blue eyes, dropped, and shook his head wondering how he ever got himself into this mess.

Andrew headed to a car borrowed from a friend to make the trip from town, when his three children caught the sight of him. Two started calling, "Daddy, wait. Don't go." His daughter stopped running and started to cry as loud as she knew how, sounding like a wounded calf. He stopped in his tracks, knowing full well he couldn't leave his little girl screaming for him. He turned around, walked toward his daughter, leaned over, and picked her up. She continued to wail so he patted her back telling her, "It will be all right." The child placed her head on her father's shoulder as she quieted to sniffling while sucking on her fingers.

Bobby ran up to his dad anxious to make plans on their trucking trip. He waited until Andrew had calmed his sister. Then his dad's attention was drawn to his brother at a nearby tree. There he was beating the tree with a stick with all his might and saying some pretty rough words. Andrew called his name saying, "Here now. You stop that you hear me, boy? — I said stop it or I'll find a switch for you." The brother dropped the stick and ran off toward the dirt road leading back to the old sharecropper's cabin. You could see the dust kicked up with his tough bare feet. It would be a while before he would come back with a face set as long as a mule.

BOBBY AND CAROLYN, SISTER

37

Bobby took his place as soon as there was a break in the commotion. "Hey Dad, you know I will be out of school soon and you said I could go with you in the truck for trip when…" Andrew stopped him before he could say another word, "I know what I said son but we will have to wait and see. I just…" Bobby jumped in this time, "Dad, I want to go with you in the truck like we talked about." His sister raised her head and in a whiney voice said, "Daddy, I want to go on a trip with you in the big truck. Please, daddy, please." Then the wailing and crying started again. Bobby tugged on his dad's shirt. Andrew placed his daughter down in the grass where she laid her head back and started kicking her feet. She yelled so loud it caused her mother to come and push open the screen door.

Andrew noticed he now had an audience. One with a smug look on her face with her mouth starting to curl up at the edges like a vulture finding a kill on the roadway. He jerked away from Bobby yanking on his shirt, turning to make his way off to the car. He slammed the door as Bobby ran up to the door saying, "So, you and I are taking off soon, right dad?" Andrew turned the keys in the ignition, "Told you boy, we need to wait and see. Now get away from the car. Get, you hear?" Bobby took a couple of steps back as he watched his dad pull away, throwing dust up as the wheels spun and turned toward the road.

Andrew promised himself he was not going to go through that anymore. No siree. He would send that woman the money some way as long as he did not have to take it to her. He had not talked to Margaret about taking Bobby in the truck. She would probably not let him go out of pure spite. Well, why bother bringing it up again? Bobby probably would forget about it anyway. He will be getting out of school and be thinking 'bout fishing. "That youngen sure 'nuff loved to fish more than anyone he had ever seen. Besides, his grandpa would talk Margaret out of letting him go even if she gave her permission. The old man doesn't like the type of people I am around so I just won't bring it up again."

Andrew put it out of his head but for the next visit arranged to get the money down early in the morning before anyone was awake. All the bills were stuffed in an envelope with the name of the smug witch (he was still married to) scrawled across the front. He crammed it in the crack of the back door then left. Relieved at not seeing any disappointed faces, of hearing any questions, or that crying and wailing, he rolled out the drive waiting to start the car until he got to the end of the drive. Andrew was not risking losing his getaway.

Bobby suddenly awoke, looked out the window of the room he shared with his brother and spotted the car his dad was driving when he had last visited rolling down the drive. He knew his dad would come after him! Bobby grabbed the bag he had packed for his trip. He pulled up a strap of his overalls over one shoulder and grabbed his boots with his free hand as he ran out the front door. His dad was on the road coming toward him. Bobby started yelling, "Here I am Dad. I'm ready." He rushed down the cement steps that took him to the road. His dad drove by the boy looking straight ahead. He did not brake. He accelerated. Bobby dropped his bag and his boots and took off like a track star running after the car, yelling for his dad to stop. He only stopped running when he no longer saw the car. Out of breath, his chest heaving, he rested bent over with his hands on his knees, spitting on the road below him. As he slowly walked back to where he dropped his belongings, he noticed how sore his feet were from his jaunt. Instead of picking his things up, he plopped down beside them on the cement steps. He just knew his dad would come back. No way that his dad saw him standing there and would just leave. He came too early, Bobby thought. Dad will be back later to pick me up. Bobby waited on those steps for three days. Yes, he would go into the house at night so he would not worry his Aunt Inez, mom, and grandfather. He didn't sleep much because he would jump up each time he heard a car, truck or even a tractor coming from either direction. On the last day sitting on those steps—he only would raise his head up as a vehicle passed in front of him. Grandfather Shinn came down and sat beside the boy. He did not say a word. He raised his arm and laid it over the boy's shoulders, grabbing on firmly to his right shoulder with his large, worn hands with knuckles knotted all up. Some fingers were straight, others bent, (evidence of years of hard work). One of those big, old hands gently shook Bobby. The boy did not need much courage, for he then let lose all his disappointment, crying hot, streaming tears leaving trails down his dusty face. His nose was running like a hose pipe. He nuzzled his straw-colored head onto his grandpa's chest, leaving dust, tears and snot all over the old man's pressed white cotton shirt. The old man firmly held on and let the child cry it all out. Grandpa Shinn knew this was a kind of a way down deep, inside hurt. No reason to bury it, best to let it go right there on Route 4 of Highway 200.

LUTHER T. SHINN,
BOBBY LEFLER'S MATERNAL GRANDFATHER

The boy lifted his head, wiped his nose on the bib of his overalls then said, "Grandpa, why did he drive right past me? He didn't even look at me. He is my dad, ain't he? Ain't he?" Grandpa Shinn nodded his head. He looked at Bobby and said in a quiet, almost whispered tone, "I want you to listen to me now." It was Bobby's turn to nod his head. "Now, I do not know the answers to the questions you are asking me. I just don't." Bobby's head dropped. His shoulders shaking as he started to cry again.

"Listen to me son. It is important that your ears hear this." Bobby straightened up his shoulders, sniffed up his nose, and looked at his grandfather eye-to-eye readying himself for the truth. The old man was impressed by this boy's inner strength now steady to take on whatever was about to come. "What I do know is, (the old man took a deep breath), this is not about you. It is not if you are a good boy or not. Your dad and mom both love you. Their hearts are not in the right place, acting selfish. I am afraid because of that, a lot of hurt, hurt like you are feeling right now is going to cut deep. I can't change it. God help me. I have prayed and prayed."

Grandpa, shaking his head, looking up toward the sky, took in a few more deep breaths. "Bobby, you have to decide right now if you are going to allow their troubles to be your troubles. Be careful now because you could drag this along the rest of your life. It will get heavier and heavier. It is hard for a boy not to be a part of the, well—cow pile those two have laid. If anyone can crawl out from under all this, it is you. I will help you all I can for as long as I am still breathing. If you decide it is your trouble too, I am telling you right here and now—It will drown you. I don't want to watch that. So, tell me, what are you gonna do with all this mess?"

Bobby was just a boy. He knew he could not fix whatever was going on. He did not know how to keep from dragging it with him either. Hurting like this was like being kicked by one of those heifers out in the pasture (and that sure ain't no fun). He knew his grandfather was waiting on an answer. He looked at him in the eye again and said, "Grandpa, I don't want to carry someone else's trouble, like you say, but I am just a boy. What do I know about staying out of their troubles?" The old man smiled and rubbed that straw-colored hair. "Boy, you are something else, you know it! That is a right smart question you asked just now. I am telling you to obey your momma and daddy. If they want to take you somewhere, wait until they are loading up the car and saying come on before you get ready to go out the door. That way there will be no misunderstandings. Understand?" Bobby replied, "I think so, but let's make a deal. If you see I am getting all wound up about something I ought not to, let me know. Will you do that for me grandpa?" The old man was proud of the boy. He might just make something out of himself despite all this commotion, he thought.

The tales of his mother being a "rounder" soon started after the news of his father's departure from the house. These stories haunted the children even more than the ones of their father. A mother spoken of in those terms was disastrous for any of her children. Bobby loved his mother dearly. He was convinced, there was nothing to all that talk. It was because she was a divorcee' and had gone out to dance a time or two. Well, there is nothing wrong with that—or was there? He knew his grandpa wouldn't approve of such a place. No way his Aunt Inez would be caught behind the dance hall doors for any reason, not even for getting out the vote, (and she was serious about that topic).

Bobby would not believe the stories the other kids told them about his mother's actions—how she was smoking and dancing with nearly every man in the place. Bobby had seen her wearing bright lipstick and her tops were tighter and skirts shorter than he had seen any other kids' mother's wear. No matter what, she was a good person and he loved her. He and his brother would take on anyone that had anything bad to say about his mother or his father. Those two became quite the scrappers. His brother would not quit a fight even when the contender was done for. Nope, Bobby would have to pull him off to keep him from knocking them to kingdom come. How does the saying go? "What does not kill you makes you stronger." That must have been referring to anyone that went against those brothers.

Siblings were an advantage in life when it seems the whole school is against you. Making friends with folks was not easy when their parents did not want them talking to you. All three of Andrew and Margaret's children were attractive, with blonde hair and the most unusual, beautiful blue eyes. Each one had a different shade of blue with Bobby's being the lightest, (ice, crystal blue). Neither of the brothers took a girl to a school dance nor was their sister asked to one. They all knew it was because of the talk, yet none of them ever said a word to anyone about it. I guess it was just another one of those family secrets kept locked up because if you can't say anything nice then don't say anything.

Decades later, Bobby met his older sister at a lodge meeting. He did not know of this sister's existence. She did know of Bobby's existence, his brother's, and his sister's (all born to Margaret and Andrew). She was a half-sister from his father's first marriage—another bit of information of which Bobby was unaware. Bobby was in his late thirties, when he came to know he was his father's second child. He was not the first born as he always thought of himself. He wondered who in his family knew of this bit of family history and what else he may not know. These family secrets can shift your view of your place in your own corner of the world.

**

INEZ SHINN WITH LUTHER T. SHINN, FATHER

California, USA — 1960

I nga would say the American language was so confusing because a word would have different meanings. The first story I recall her using was when the ship she was serving on docked in California. The staff were allowed to disembark and go ashore for a few days of leave.

Inga was enthralled with any opportunity to explore, especially America. It was a place that so many talked about with its grand inventions, Hollywood's glamour and—add to it—Rock and Roll (the golden opportunities for all that sought it).

Inga split the fare of a taxi from the docks to the downtown area with a couple of shipmates. She chose to walk around the town of Long Beach instead of going on with a couple of friends that would most likely end up in a local bar. All bars begin to look the same making it difficult to tell where you have been if that is the only thing you have seen. No, she wanted to see what these Americans were up to and why everyone was so excited.

Inga popped into a coffee shop. It was loud. All the customers were speaking English, no other languages heard. The dishes were clanging into sinks with silverware clashing on top. Cups were clattering with the saucers. A large man was yelling out and ringing a bell and waitresses were yelling back across the small space.

The establishment had bulky, vinyl, upholstered bench seats with high backs that felt like they swallowed you when you slid in to sit down. The smooth surface table edged in what looked like chrome from the wheel of a car was centered between the bulging seats.

She waited for direction when one of the waitresses said, "Honey, find yourself a place to take a load off," as she pointed to a long stretch of chairs hooked to a shorter bar type area. There you could eat, read the newspaper, and smoke a cigarette all while sipping coffee. The food was more than a pastry and fruit. No wonder the Americans are so strong, she thought to herself. They eat a full meal to start the day with meat, eggs, and pancakes. It was several minutes before the same woman came by and asked her what she was having. Inga, a bit startled by the pace of the place mouthed, "Just coffee please."

The young Norwegian looked about the place as she sipped the coffee that was packed with a jolt. There were no cloth linens draped over the table or cloth napkins folded in a fanned-out fashion holding the silverware. The tables were wiped with a damp cloth once the dishes were removed from the previous customer, a crude environment without a doubt. It was certainly, no match for the civility demanded in the cruise ship's dining areas including the one set aside for the staff only.

The day's adventure had started out with a bang. She left coins for the coffee and a little extra for the waitress which she knew was a customary thing to do. She slid down from her perch on the swinging chairs which felt like she was dismounting some sort of playground apparatus for children. Over-caffeinated and/or stimulated, the explorer headed out the glass-swinging door to see what else awaited in this land of grab and go.

Once outside, Inga noticed she had not left the noise inside the shoppe'. It seemed to have followed her as a stray cat might if it smelled tuna wafting from her shoes. The source of this unsettling racket was cars. There were so many vehicles; some on the road either coming or going, others parked in front of the stores. She had not seen this many cars in one place—ever.

Many ports of call had a few taxi cabs and maybe one or two cars for those that were of some importance to be driven to their hotels. Other places may have bicycles with a peddler and a wagon for one to two people to tour a city, much like the purpose of a rickshaw pulled by a man. It seemed here there was a car to every person.

She walked for several blocks as she was attempting to keep up with the rate of her heart, realizing she was almost at a trot. Her feet were aching. She had become breathless from being quite overwhelmed. She had not slowed down to take a look around due to her frenzied state.

Inga noticed a string of several stores with large glass windows. She pulled on one of the heavy doors and entered into a family clothing store. There, right in front, was a diagram of the sections in the store. The last listing indicated a "Rest Room," in the back far left corner of the store. "Why that is just what I need. How nice the Americans are to have a place to sit down and rest when you are tired from shopping," she thought to herself. It would be wonderful to take her shoes off and just sit for a few or more minutes. Inga rushed past the racks of women's clothing, turned left at the shoe department which was difficult not to stop and linger for she loved to look at shoes. The children's department was to her left and the infants to her right when she noted the sign above the door—Restroom. Quickly she scooted across the linoleum floor ignoring a shelf stacked with baby bottles, bumping it ever so slightly. Thank goodness nothing fell. There she was in front of the door. There was a restroom for men and one for women. She thought women did most of the shopping. Why did men need a room to rest in? Oh well, maybe in America men helped with shopping.

Inga pushed open the door expecting to see a couch or two, and maybe a few chairs with a soft rug on the floor. She was astonished at the view of four sinks on the right wall and a wall of doors on the opposite wall. Thinking, maybe the chairs are over on the other side, she walked further into the room, viewing four more doors in line next to one another. Curious and in need of a place to kick off these shoes if for only a few minutes, she pushed open the first door. There behind the door was a toilet—place to relieve oneself. Quickly, going from one door to the next only to find—toilets! "I thought this was a room to rest, not a room to urinate and other such stuff!" Desperate and seeing no one else in the "Rest" room, Inga went into the toilet room, covered the seat and sat down, sliding her shoes off with a sigh of relief.

Years later she used this tale as an example of the fact that though Americans may be known around the world for saying what they mean and meaning what they say, it did not apply to words akin to restroom.

MY MOTHER'S SUITCASE

Inga kept a list of words she found confusing or comical on the back page of her notebook. One of those she had listed and marveled when she first saw the United States had a state with the name Virginia. She thought Americans must be fond of women to name an entire state after an intimate female body part, (Vagina). She laughed adding there were many words that were similar, a few even the same yet had different meanings. Admitting it could be very confusing and embarrassing at times.

She had bought a small overnight suitcase to match the one she had when she first went to sea. The smaller one held her notebook, souvenirs, and letters. They both had keys but she only locked the smaller one because it had her personal thoughts written in the notebook.

**

A Cure or a Bandaid

*Two broken people will either fit together perfectly
or destroy each other beyond repair*

BOBBY AND INGA 1960

MY MOTHER'S SUITCASE

Long Beach, California in the United States of America is where Inga, a young, pretty, fair skinned woman from Norway with dark hair and dark eyes met a handsome American, blonde haired man with crystal ice blue eyes. He was a U.S. Navy sailor from the state of North Carolina in the American south. Already having something in common as both spent much of their time out at sea, the two were set up by friends and spent much of the first date dancing. Although they did not know it yet, there was the shared experience of disappointing childhoods, and parents who failed them in some way. Two people that were not the best choices to marry one another— neither coming from stable, loving back grounds not to mention to have children of their own when they themselves were not blessed with the best role models on parenting.

The marriage of a man and a woman with more than average challenges in their families of origin; could it be that there was hope that familial history would not repeat itself? What could have the expectations been? Were their expectations high, because they would be different from what was viewed in their own parent's marriages? Did they believe in love through whatever obstacles may come their way? Did they perhaps have little to no expectation and thought to just roll the dice and hope for the best (and if it goes sour than divorce and go to your own corner to start over again)?

It could be each offered the other something they needed. Bobby wanted something beyond what was offered in rural North Carolina. He also wanted to be the hero in someone's life. Who better than a virtual orphan from a country recovering from war?

Inga needed someone to offer a place to call home, stability, and strength to protect her from the ugliness she had so far experienced in her world. An American military man who spoke proudly of his extended family that was handsome and liked to dance would be a tempting prospect.

The most probable scenario is the young couple met up in a bar with friends. They both were docked while serving on a ship and it was time for a little rest and relaxation. They danced a little, talked less, finding out the things that may fit the need from the other and they had sex—a lot of sex. They were both intrigued. One thing led to another and possibly he was going to be deployed. It could be they did not want to separate yet and the only solution was marriage. It would not be the first time one of the most important decisions in life was made influenced more by hormones and the joy of the physical pleasures.

Another story once spun was the tale that Inga trapped Bobby into marriage telling him she was pregnant, so he had to marry her. When they married, she was not pregnant, so she made sure to become pregnant as quickly as possible. Yes, this is a possibility, given a child was born ten months and sixteen days after the marriage date.

They married soon and had two pretty, little girls with golden hair. Their love story lacked many details and did not paint a picture in my head as the one launching dishes into the sea had done. It was not the fairy tale young girls giggle at when it is told over and over again. It could be this page just wasn't colored in. It is as if someone started with a crayon, then found another page more interesting.

***

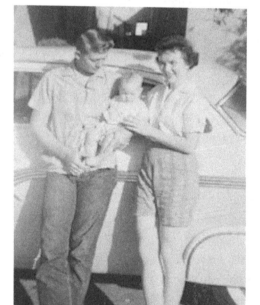

BOBBY AND INGA WITH FIRST BORN, WANDA 1961

Overseas Deployment Family Included

JAPAN

One of the most perplexing questions I, or most military brats, must answer is simple for most people. "Where are you from?" How do you respond? Is it the place you were born but left before you developed even the faintest memory? Is it the place you started school? Perhaps, the best answer is the duty station that your family stayed at the longest or the last one where you resided. Maybe it was the place where one of your parents grew up and that you visited for most of the holidays.

The answers will be different as the reasons for the answers vary. The children of military parents are lovingly called "military brats" in all the branches of service. Our symbol is the dandelion, appropriately so, because we are blown with the wind all over the world depending on the parents next duty station.

The first place I have memories of is Japan. My father was able to bring his family due to the length of deployment. I was about eighteen months, and my sister was an infant. I have a few recollections. Oddly, I can remember the layout of our housing unit. There were two bedrooms upstairs. The living room, dining room and kitchen would be very popular these days with it all being open space.

I recall watching cartoons and where the television was in the living room. My sister crawled around the open space trying to bite me with her newly obtained teeth. I screeched and ran circles around the coffee table to avoid her sharp teeth sinking into my legs.

I was allowed to go outside to escape her for a little while. There was a patio where I could ride a tricycle. Mom brought out a snack of Hostess snowballs. You may remember the pink colored, coconut covered chocolate cupcake with white cream center that came in a package of two. My mother told me that I always shared my pack, giving a local homeless man one of my cupcakes.

Unfortunately, I cannot remember being altruistic so early or even the man himself. It may have been too traumatic. Mom asked if I remembered the walk one day when we saw him floating in the river. He had drowned. Some memories do not need to be thought of and seeing a drowned body tops the list.

Dad was stationed in Japan for possibly three years. There was an annual event in which the Japanese memorialized when the atomic bombs were dropped on Hiroshima and Nagasaki, August 6 and 9. The Japanese government paid for the farmers to come from the fields to picket the American installations. I had a prime viewing on one such occasion from my parent's second story bedroom window in navy housing. There was a group of men walking around with large signs on sticks and lit torches. They were chanting, "Yankee Go Home," repeatedly. Their voices became louder, and it seemed like they would never go away. I sat at the top of the stairs in our unit holding a baby doll. When my mother came to check on me, I had cut all the hair off my doll with a pair of children's blunt ended scissors. Mom did not scold me. She sat beside me, collected the scissors, the poor bald doll, and told me those men would soon be gone. She added they were not going to hurt us as she was scooping up the doll hair snipping's in her other hand. She reminded me there was a tall fence with guards nearby.

We sat there until the voices quieted. She walked me back to the window so we could see they had left. I asked her what they had been saying. She told me. I asked her who did they want to go home? She told me the farmers came once a year to tell the Americans to go home because they did not want them there. Not understanding why, as little children will do, I questioned why they did not like us. Her reply, "Who knows why men fight, but they do," urging me to come with her downstairs to start supper. She added as an afterthought, "You need not worry, we will not be here next year when they do it."

There were also rare and special, "me and daddy moments" while we lived in Japan. My mom shared with me, but I do not remember them at all. I do not have a photograph or even a hint of it occurring. Evidently, Dad had a motorcycle. He seated me in front of him, placed my tiny body between his arms and legs and putted around in the mornings. I did not know this daddy that was patient and gentle. Oh, how I wish I could have a blink of Bobby and I on the motorcycle.

The little I know of economics, despite being in the military, we must have lived as if we were royalty while in Japan. A nice lady came in and helped my mom a couple of days a week. She was teaching me simple words of Japanese and, no, I do not know any of the language. She had me call her "Mamasan." Oh, how robustly she would laugh with full smile and throwing her head back whenever I said it.

Most of our household goods were purchased while we were in Japan. It is where our dishes, furniture, the television, and the stereo were bought. I heard Dad say it cost less so he could buy more of what we needed.

My white suitcase was from a set dad and mom purchased while we were residing in Japan. The matching white Lady Baltimore suitcases—two large ones and two somewhat smaller ones so each member of our family of four would have one. It was odd that the suitcases came from a country without a city named Baltimore. It must have been imported from the United States for sale at the navy exchange.

Funny now thinking of my dad carrying a suitcase with the insignia of, "Lady Baltimore" in thick, gold, metal script glued to the outside. I guess there was not one with a tag of, "Baltimore Sailor, Mister Baltimore or more to his liking— Soon to be Chief Baltimore," to glue on his rectangular box. I have no doubt he would have preferred it that way.

I kept my little suitcase well into adulthood, storing things that my children had made over the years. The contents were remnants of happy times. There were construction paper turkeys made from drawings of little handprints, paper folded in half wishing for a Happy Mother's Day and Norwegian baskets woven from giftwrap that once dangled from our family Christmas tree.

***

WANDA, AGE 3 DRESSED IN JAPANESE ATTIRE

Appearances are Important

"Your name is the most important thing you own.
Don't ever do anything to disgrace or cheapen it."
—BEN HOGAN, BEN HOGAN QUOTES AND SAYINGS

I am the older sister of two girls in my family. There were no brothers, which meant no boys, or, more importantly, no sons born to my daddy. I do not know how my sister, Selma felt about it. For me, I always felt like I had disappointed my dad for having been born a girl. I did not feel too awful about it because I was quite a prissy little girl. My mother said she had got just what she wanted, two little girls.

I was named Wanda by my father. If it sounds country, it is. I was told he chose the name after the Queen of Rockabilly, (that he was wild for—Wanda Jackson). Look her up, she was billed as the female Elvis. I kid you not.

Side Note: I consider Elvis my first crush. My mom would let me take a nap during the day to stay up later to watch one of his movies on the TV set later in the evening. When my parents were not in the room, I scooted up close to the set and kissed him on the screen. I was only six. Elvis was handsome, sang so differently and he danced! I kind of liked my name, once I learned that little tidbit of being named after a woman noted as the female Elvis.

My dad also chose my middle name of Lynn. It was not until I was at the age of fifty-two, that I awoke one morning finally making the connection, that my middle name was from one of Bobby's former girlfriends. Yippee! I do not know when my mother or my Great Aunt and other family noticed. No one, not even my mother, ever mentioned it to me.

Well, fate being what it is, at least I could not be a constant reminder of either, for I did not have dark hair and creamy pale skin. The strong attraction to women with these physical traits seemed to plague my daddy like a deadly vice. If they needed to be rescued, the stronger the passion.

Yes, my sister, although born the second child, took on the tradition of being named after women in the family. Selma was my mother's mom and Inez was my dad's eldest aunt. I never inquired if it was my father's or my mother's decision regarding the names.

My father's mother, given the moniker of Abigail Margaret, was also called "Babe," due to her birth order as the youngest of four daughters. I am certain Babe found the name choice of Selma Inez not to her liking in the least, for it did not honor her. If Inga chose the name, then she gained an enemy in the Shinn–Lefler family court for a lifetime. If she did not choose the name, I am certain she would have been blamed for doing so, regardless of if she or Dad assigned the honors.

Ironically, my sister Selma did not care for the tradition that gifted her the names. She did not think it was any great honor at all. She spent years scribbling other names for herself all over anything that would take to ink.

This was particularly true for the cover of our telephone book. If you lived in the 1960's–1970's, to locate a phone number you flipped pages of names in alphabetical order in a thick, large paper book. Everyone in the area had the same carrier. The phone company (what we called this entity) provided the phone books. The pages were yellow in the back section. These were businesses listed by the type of service or care provided.

If my sister did not have enough space on the cover of the phone book for a newly concocted label for herself, she started tagging the yellow pages with her large loopty–loos. I believe some handwriting expert had said on a crime TV show that handwriting that was large and flowing with lavish looping may indicate that one may have exaggerated thoughts of one's own grandeur. Well, based on the name choices and combinations scrawled all over, I tend to agree with the TV expert. Oh, by the way, none of those name combinations included any part of my dad's mother's name.

My daddy, Bobby Henderson Lefler spent his life attempting to have people to think of him in a most favorable light. My guess is he wanted to be considered respectable with no scandal attached to the Lefler name in his charge. The cliché' "Appearances are important", would be a gross understatement. The cliché' is more a mantra in the B.H. Lefler handbook of life. He spent a tremendous amount of time assuring our car was clean. My mother laundered and pressed his clothes. Bobby's daughters' faces were clean, hair combed, clothes fit appropriately and mended if needed. My sister and I were instructed to have shoes on when we were outside. My dad did not like for us to be barefooted for some reason. Flip flops were the accepted bare minimum.

The place we lived in was to be tidy. He held inspection on Saturday mornings before leaving for the race car shop. He had a list for each weekday with the chores assigned to Selma and me. This included, "Police the front lawn", which he explained was to pick up any of *his* cigarette butts that may be on the grass. We were called out to attend to any infraction, required to rectify the matter and then we could move on.

A part of this obsessive-compulsive check list was fueled by his brain influenced by the military. It was instilled in family as a whole, by not-so-subtle methods. A prime example is the navy has a store called, "The Exchange." It was much like any retail store offering clothing and household goods. The exchange was always located on the navy base providing these goods to service members at a better price than the civilian retail stores. There was a community board at the entrance that people could place announcements such as upcoming events at the base or items they may have for sale.

A particular base we resided, chose to place snapshots of naval housing units on the community board with the number of the unit listed on the photo. The purpose was direct and to the point. It was to shame those living in those units. A few of the photos were of trash cans left out past the designated trash pick-up day or tipped over spilling garbage onto the lawn. Another photo showed bikes thrown down on the front sidewalk or too many items stacked up in the back of the unit.

My dad pointed out the board, adding that he never wanted to see our unit photo posted there. He reiterated it is why he would stay after us girls, to put up our bikes before we came into our unit. He made it clear it would not look good to his commanders. My eyes would frantically search for our unit number on our way into the exchange every time. I wondered too, how unfair it was if the wind had blown down someone's garbage can and their unit is posted on the board. And if you are asking yourself if our unit was ever posted on the board, of course not!

I would being slack if I did not share an incident of how my mother's attitude of, "Do not worry about it. At least the bombs aren't dropping", collided with my dad's regimented lifestyle of, "Everything being squared away." Dad was getting ready for work when his button to his uniform pants popped off. He could not find the button. Mom reassured him she could find a button in her button box and sew it on quickly to avoid him being late. *Being prompt is another story in itself.* She did as she was asked, sewing on the button and he was calm and out the door in no time. Several hours passed and I was home from school. Mom was cooking dinner when dad arrived home. He asked if she remembered that he had inspection that morning. *(He was the one being inspected. His appearance from his cover (Hat) to the shine on his shoes and everywhere in between was scrutinized.)* Mom began laughing uncontrollably. My sister and I usually did not listen to the conversations between the two because at the time it was not of much interest to us. The laughter however piqued our attention as we scurried into the kitchen.

Mom with an apron tied around her waist and a large spoon in one hand was bent over trying to catch her breath because she was laughing so much. When we asked why she was laughing and what was so funny, mom was pointing toward dad's tummy. Dad was standing there rolling those blue eyes not amused in the least. She clearly was so overwhelmed with amusement that she could not answer our ever-pressing questions. She only pointed and laughed more. Dad showed us his button on his pants, to be seen only if his gleaming brass buckle from his belt was loosened. The button was not the regulation khaki color. No, it was an ivory color and the shape of a bunny. Yes, mom knew of the inspection but still she chose a rabbit shaped button to sew to replace the popped of regulation button.

Selma and I looked at dad before we dared to giggle. He cracked a slight smile and said it was a good thing no one else had noticed it because of the belt buckle. He only noticed a few minutes before the inspection then it was too late to do anything about it. This stirred mom's hilarity into high gear. He requested, in an order type voice, to not ever do that again.

***

SHINN SISTERS

BESSIE INEZ, MARGARET ABIGAIL, LAURA MAE

Coming Home to the U.S. and Aunt Inez

1965

My sister and I had not been seen by extended family, except for photos. In part due to being born in California, the other coast from my dad's family in North Carolina. Our little family soon transferred to Japan after Selma was born. I was four years old, and Selma was three years old, when we returned to the states heading to Cabarrus County to be introduced to dad's family.

Our first stop was at the family's homeplace. My great-grandfather built the house to raise his family with my great-grandmother. They had four girls (one that died at age 4 from tonsilitis). The eldest daughter remained residing at the homeplace after her father passed away.

She was a fine woman by the name of Inez Shinn. I knew her as my Great Aunt Inez. I took to her as soon as I met her. I sat on her lap, not wanting to scoot off. I loved being with her. Her house sat on farmland that once had orchards and acres of rows of all types of vegetables. The cattle still grazed behind the fence posts cut from trees off the land. The crops raised were needed to keep the family fed. The remainder was sold to support the family. Evidently, the farm was operated successfully enough to have two daughters attend and obtain a degree in education at a nearby college in the 1920's.

Aunt Inez did tell many family stories. She also participated in acts of omission by leaving any of the information with as much as a pinch of negative reflection on either side of the family. The reality of situations, without use of rose-colored glasses, were pieced together from observations, stories told and retold including the unsaid words.

Aunt Inez was the keeper of the family records, including dates of births, deaths, marriages, and any landmark moments a member of the family may accomplish. She wrote announcements of the people on the eastern end of Cabarrus County for the local newspaper. Of course, announcements of the members of St. Martin Lutheran Church were penned by her for the bulletin each Sunday.

Miss Inez, as many referred to her, was considered the historian in eastern Cabarrus County region with good reason. She had an excellent memory with attention to detail. She kept the records written in her papers. Unfortunately, her papers were not kept in any type of suitcase but in boxes stacked here, there, and everywhere. This could pose an issue when searching for a particular set of papers because the boxes place on top of one another and not labeled.

She lived alone but she was never lonely for she was always on the phone speaking to other community leaders every evening. She wrote not only for her church and the local newspaper but faithfully wrote letters to those that may be recovering from an illness or had a recent loss of a family member. It was common for her to write letters of encouragement and concern to her congressman, her senator, and the president of the United States.

She also wrote letters to our little family wherever we were stationed. Mom would read them to us at bedtime. Sis and I looked forward to seeing the drawings at the bottom of the letter. The simple drawings were of a rabbit, cat, or the dog she loved.

My grandmother, Abigail Margret Shinn Lefler Hartsell was the youngest sister of Inez. I watched how Abigail would talk to her sister, Inez and how she talked about her when she was not around. Despite me being a young girl, I thought my grandmother was jealous of my Great Aunt Inez. Possibly for her standing in the community or any of a hundred other small benign reasons sisters often hold onto with all their might. Reasons I have no knowledge of, yet I can speculate that my sister, Selma Inez, being crowned as a namesake of my mother's mother and Great Aunt Inez did not impress my grandmother, Miss Abigail not one iota.

Family secrets ran rampant in my dad's family. The knowing of a secret, no matter how small or life altering, was power. The smallest item given from one family member to another was accompanied with the promise of utmost secrecy. *As if it was to be protected like a top secret from the Pentagon and releasing the information would be met with swift and severe consequences.* "Now here you take this but do not tell anybody. You hear no one is to know."

There were many unspoken rules. The goal was not to cause those involved any further harm. It instead caused hurt feelings and misunderstandings that lasted for years. The ones that knew the particulars did not speak of the details. Then there were some that were not allowed to know. It was terribly confusing to not know the who, what, when and how of your family's history.

As much as I loved my Aunt Inez, her marital status was a mystery to me until I was an adult. Another member in the family in a hush, hush, whispered conversation explained that indeed Aunt Inez had been married. He was already married to another woman. He used the funds gained from my dearest aunt to open a restaurant in a nearby town.

Upon finding out about this man's deceit, Aunt Inez shut the restaurant down, refusing to sell it to any buyer for decades. Yes, I said *decades*. The brick restaurant with main street road frontage stood empty as a silent reminder of the consequences of the careless act of wronging an intelligent woman.

What was more puzzling is why she carried his last name attached to hers to her death. I thought the second marriage would be null and void for a bigamist already married to one person. I guess that pride thing will make you hang with a name for years and years. How can it be better than having to admit someone betrayed your trust and stole from you? She punished herself, not by adorning a scarlet A, but by signing his last name every time she wrote out a check. Anytime she was introduced to someone it was his last name said out loud. It seems to me that would prolong the conversation about the indiscretion.

Aunt Inez's marriage or not really marriage, was one of many secrets. I am sure I will not know most of the ones clamped down tightly between lips of the mouths of my daddy's family. Here is an example how an incident can change from what occurred to what sounds better. My grandmother married a second time. This man had a newspaper route. He would have to leave in the early hours while it was still dark out. There were papers to pick up, advertisements to add then roll the paper, place a rubber band around to hold all in place. If it was raining, the papers had to be placed in a plastic wrapping to keep them dry when tossed on lawns and drives. It was a must to have them delivered before people awoke in the mornings. Well, he was involved in a single vehicle accident that totaled his truck. I was staying with Aunt Inez when the call came through informing her that he had been taken to the hospital in bad condition. Although being around the age of ten, I could under-stand the one-way conversation. The caller provided the affirmation of Aunt Inez's suspicions that indeed he had been drinking, because a liquor bottle was found in the truck. By the time the talking was over, it was decided the story was to go that he had fallen asleep behind the wheel, lost control of the truck and crashed.

A particular story I did hear as a child was more serious in nature than bigamy or a drunkard crashing his truck. Although, it is not my story to tell, I have shared it with an elder member to prevent it remaining a family secret hidden in a dark closet. The principal ones in the awful acts knew when it occurred and allowed it to continue. Why, you wonder? It was due to their selfish needs. Maybe they feared repercussions, yet they walked and talked in the stinking, nasty swamp right along with the one that did the deed. Whenever I go by the cemetery where many of our family are at eternal rest, I locate a certain granite grave marker lain flat in the ground so as not to bother a lawn mower. Thick, lush, green grass lines the marker and the large headstone. A stomp or two on top of that piece of granite to let that ole lech know, the secret is not safe and not kept. It makes me feel better.

Is it any wonder some of us had trouble making decisions as we studied issues in our lives? Simple problems could be hashed over dozens of times, taking days to solve. You never knew if you truly had been provided with enough information to make a decisive conclusion. Second guessing most decisions is natural. Then second guessing the decision once it had been beaten to particles of dust if some-thing—anything went wrong.

***

Tends to Flowers and Children

A suitcase on roller skates would have been really, helpful when we visited my daddy's family in North Carolina during the 1960's and '70's. There was a handle in the middle of the two latches that helped you lug it out of the car. Being a tiny girl (you know you are tiny if you are always sitting on the front row of the class pictures at school) it took both hands wrapped tightly, pinching some fingers together, while it felt more like squeezing than holding the handle to pick up the rectangular box. One step taken at a time—sliding the other foot to the one moving forward, banging your legs below the knees so that later you have blue and purple up and down one lower leg.

It was an awkward task, but I was not risking my stuff being left in the trunk when my parents took off. I did not ask my dad to retrieve it either because heaven forbid it would have slowed him down from getting where he was going. The Chief would have been huffing and puffing like the wolf in the story of, "The Three Little Pigs." Once, we arrived in Cabarrus County, mom and dad would drop me off with my Great Aunt Inez. I would not see or hear from them until it was time to load up my suitcase in the trunk of our GTO to return to South Carolina.

My great-aunt's house was a place of wonder and magic. I was always enthralled at the homeplace of the Shinn's. Stories of gold hunts, picking flowers, or learning how to sew from the scraps of material left over from cutting out a dress for a family member. Learning to thread needle and knotting it to start a simple stitch provided a great feeling of accomplishment.

I have never met anyone with a greener thumb than my aunt. I believed all she had to do was put a hole in the hard red clay, plop a plant or seed in it and it would grow like the fabled beanstalk. There was a plethora of flowers in a myriad of colors planted all around the house and barn.

Given she was a schoolteacher, she had an immense supply of crayons, paints, brushes, and plenty of paper to create masterpieces. Did I mention she did not fuss about a possible mess? Well, she did not stand around on raw nerves telling you to be careful not to spill or splash. Her approach was encouraging and inspired originality.

Oh, let us not forget, Aunt Inez's pound cakes, so light with a bit of a crunchy crust, her cakes were known as the best around. She did not mind if we chose to eat the cake for breakfast. It was she who first introduced Sis and I to the making of Jell-O—stirring hot water into the gelatin powder until it was dissolved. The hardest thing was waiting for it to cool off in the refrigerator enough to eat it.

Jiffy popcorn came in an aluminum pan to be placed onto a stove burner, moving it from side to side by the wire handle until the popping slowed. The aluminum pan expanded on the top into a cone shape, once cooled a bit, to open for a yummy treat. We made banana sandwiches with peanut butter. So many things she encouraged us to try that built confidence in young girls.

Once our family was located on the east coast we spent Christmas, Easter and up to two weeks of the summer with my dad's family in North Carolina. It was always my choice to go to my dear Aunt Inez's.

There was not an ornament dangling from a tree, or a stocking hung. Yet, the spirit of Christmas was all around us. Aunt Inez shared the story of Jesus's birth and at Easter the sacrifice of his life.

Many dozens of eggs were purchased from a local grocery store along with the pellets of egg dye and the vinegar to set it. We would talk, giggle and at times burst into loud laughter with no one correcting or shushing us. Aunt Inez provided us with the supplies and the space to be creative and explore. The hours spent around that wooden kitchen table having fun are the best spent in my life.

She left her influence on me and a vast number of her family and students. An amazing woman ahead of her times. Yes ma'am, a woman that certainly changed her corner of the world.

$$***$$

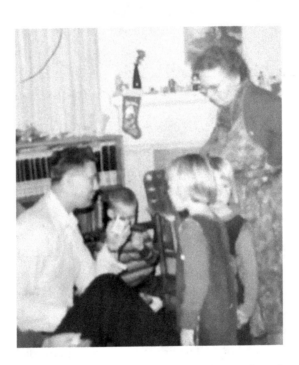

BOBBY, MIKE PLUMMER (COUSIN) WANDA, SELMA, AUNT INEZ
CHRISTMAS 1966

The Anchors for those that Serve

Behind every strong soldier,
there is an even stronger family who stands by them,
supports them and loves them with all their hearts.
—UNKNOWN, LITTLETHINGS.COM

No one is going to become wealthy on a military payroll. My mother would work as a waitress to help with extra money. My father was not fond of the idea of needing his wife to work to make ends meet. Anyone from a military family knows, if able and willing, the family helps.

I was fortunate to find letters and post cards dated from 1958, in a trunk upstairs at my dear Aunt's house. The first letters were from my daddy at the age of nineteen to twenty years old. The correspondence was written while on the ship to his grandfather and Aunt Inez. The next letters were a fair mixture to and from Aunt Inez, Bobby, and Inga. It was evident Aunt Inez and her father, Luther T. Shinn, were assisting the young couple in managing bills and at times helping them out when needed.

Soon the letters discussed the arrival of their first daughter—my dad and mom becoming parents. Mom wrote how excited Dad was, always rushing home from work to hold and look at his new little girl. She even mentioned him being in the labor room but had to leave because he became sick watching Mom in labor. The letters were reassuring that at some space and time they actually cared for one another—loved one another. Mom wrote in one letter that, "Bobby had been so sweet to help her around the house during the last weeks of pregnancy."

It was very evident that my mother and Aunt Inez had established a good relationship. This may have also fallen on Abigail's ears causing a rift between the mother-in-law and daughter-in-law prior to a relationship developing. Also, the mother-in-law having a strong liking for another young woman at home in North Carolina, waiting for her sailor son to marry her.

Great Aunt Inez would take us to downtown Concord to JC Penney, and Belks to purchase our school clothes once a year. It probably added to the twin questions since our clothes were bought in different colors yet the same style. Selma always had clothes that were blue, and it best not cause her to itch, or she would not wear it. The fits she would throw until someone would cut out a tag that dared to make her back itch!

My clothes were one of two colors, pink or green. The reason for the assigned colors was not due to our eye, hair, or skin coloring. My Great Aunt's favorite colors were pink and green. As noted, I was assigned clothes pink and green for an unsaid reason, that I favored that dear woman.

My sister Selma had the favor of all grandchildren from my dad's mother, our grandmother. Do I need to tell you that her favorite color was blue as was my father's? It was our Great Aunt that paid for our clothes whether store bought or home sewn. I do not think the color swatch for each girl was anyone else's decision but our Great Aunt's unless she listened to my mother's input. Mom was always along for the clothes shopping and the choosing of material for the seamstress to create clothes for the girls who appeared to be twins.

The clothes shopping and stopping every few feet for the adoration of the women perusing the store at the same time, was not the best of times. My sister and I being so close in age and in size were often asked, "Are you twins?" We responded in unison, "No, we are sixteen months apart." It was annoying to answer smiling strangers, mostly women, all dressed up with hats on their heads and pointed, high heeled shoes clicking as they walked toward you. They would bend down so low to look at us closely. Their dresses so tight it would not have surprised anyone looking at this scene if the stitches would have given way like exploding confetti in a hero's parade.

Of course, nothing would have fallen out because of all the under garments women were required to wear in those days. A dress was to be worn with a slip covering a bra, probably a girdle worn over your panties to keep your tummy from sticking out and to hold up the nylons nicely on your legs. Oh yes, do not forget the adornment of a perfectly placed hat upon coiffed hair, styled once a week at the beauty parlor. Gloves draped over the handbag matching those high heels was a necessity. It was pulled all together with a strand of pearls, earrings and a brooch pinned to your dress or sweater depending on the season.

No need to wonder why the Women's Movement made the cover photo on the magazines, there was often a circle of women throwing their bras into a fire.

If we behaved by staying where we could be seen or Selma not raising cane trying on a material not comfortable to her sensitive skin, we would be taken to lunch. The pharmacy was within walking distance from the stores downtown. The doors were very heavy so an adult would have to push them although we would help pushing the lower part of the thick glass door with brass handles. The tiled black and white mosaic floor was most noticeable. The pharmacist was located behind a counter in the back. There were shelves to the right and a smaller section on the left held all kind of remedies for what may ail a body. Most of the left side had a long counter with bar stools for patrons to order pastries, sandwiches, dips of ice cream and milk shakes. All the equipment for mixing those thick shakes sitting in front of a huge, mirrored glass made the place appear much larger.

When we entered the pharmacy there were greetings, introductions and asking about the welfare of the family. All of this was a social expectation that was most assuredly met before any orders for food could be given. The idea of the height-challenged Great Aunt Inez attempting a bar stool was ludicrous. We would wait, if necessary, for a table. Usually, it was not a long wait. Sis and I enjoyed walking around the store giggling at some of the things we noticed. When we happened upon mercurochrome, both of us turned on our heels moving promptly to the table. We seated ourselves as proper young ladies with napkins in our laps and were careful not to place our elbows on the table. We knew also, not to interrupt the adults when they were talking. Selma knew not to do her smacking and opening her mouth full of food to stick her tongue out, to be gross. No ma'am, not at this table with Aunt Inez and mom sitting so close. They would surely see such an inappropriate display.

Now that we were seated, served, and had eaten most of our lunch, ice cream would be allowed. Dining out for lunch felt like a grown-up activity. If that were not special enough, on some of the outings we would be able to choose an item from the store. There was a small section of items for children to peruse. Selma and I usually picked out bubble bath in bottles shaped like a Disney Princess. She chose Cinderella and I picked Snow White.

The excitement to wait for an evening bath time caused too much unrest. We would climb in Great Aunt Inez's deep claw foot tub for a bubble bath before dinner.

***

That Damn Stove

The military family has a lifestyle comparable to that of nomads. Suitcases come in handy when you traipse from place to place. Daddy, a career navy man, could receive orders at any given time. The cause and effect like the ocean tide, if you will excuse the pun, was a predictable succession of actions. Dad would come home with a pronouncement of said, "Given orders to relocate to *fill in the blank.*" In the next day or week, a green and yellow Mayflower moving truck would pull up. The Mayflower men were like a precision machine neatly packing our few belongings. Each box labeled of contents and what room they belonged in. The Mayflower truck then would travel to Dad's next duty station. He usually had to report before we arrived. Leaving Mom, the responsibility for the move.

Mom always left our unit as neat as can be. I remember many a time she was mopping up the floor on our way out the door. Mom's goal, as we scurried to leave, was to arrive in time to direct the movers where to place the boxes at the next place. The laborious chore of unpacking and placing our stuff commenced. There was not any help with this glorious event. It was just Mom, Selma, and me.

A box would be emptied. Next, all the wrapping paper was folded, to be used for some project later. The boxes were flattened and stacked in a specific place in the room. It was such a pleasure when the stack of flat boxes became higher than the number of boxes sitting in a room yet to be unpacked. Then it was on to the next room. It made so much sense not to drag stuff all over if you did not use it. Imagine all the work it was to pack, unwrap, place, just to do it all over again. The trick was if it had not been used since the last move to donate it to a local charity or the base thrift shop.

Yep, it was Mom directing two little girls, "Take this and put it over there, be careful now. Go to the kitchen and get me some paper towels so we can clean as we go along." She would not only get our unit squared away, but it was also her handling all manner of items on a lengthy checklist. The list was much more detailed when Dad had gone out to sea or to use the appropriate term—been deployed.

More than once, Dad was away from home for months at a time. On a couple of those occasions, we lived in North Carolina to be near my dad's family. Mom did not have family in the U.S. If we needed help at least we had Dad's people close.

A deployment longer than most resulted in renting an older house across the street from Aunt Inez. It was a small place quite different than the navy housing apartment units we were accustomed to living in. It was not as squared away. The most positive thing I can say about the cold, little house was the location.

It was cold and damp. There were no children or playgrounds, just a large yard with a creepy car shed and a creepier large barn. The place had no stove. All hell, broke loose—*please forgive me for she was a spiritual woman*—when my Great Aunt Inez bought a stove for my mom to use. If mom would have had the funds to buy the stove, she would have bought the stove.

My father's mom (my grandmother) was the loudest one against such a purchase. There were multiple phones calls to and from grandmother and Carolyn (Dad's sister), and of course to verbally browbeat Aunt Inez. I would not doubt that dad received multiple letters on ship regarding, "The Stove Incident." I guess my grandmother and Aunt Carolyn would just assume we eat cereal, sandwiches and get a hot plate. Aunt Inez would eat with us many evenings. The others did not earn her teacher's paycheck and had no business butting in with how she chose to spend it.

My Aunt Inez was a tremendous help to my mother by pitching in and watching us when she could. I recall going to school with her a few times. I enjoyed her third-grade students making such a fuss over me. They would talk about which one of them would sit next to me during lunch or walk in line and hold my hand.

Needless to say, taking your four-year-old great niece to school with you daily could not continue, although I would not have complained at all. My mom had a part time job at a restaurant. She located a day care not too far from her work. She dropped Selma and I off when she went to the work. Thank goodness it was not every day and there were other children to play with outside.

One evening, Mom had to stay later at work for some reason. It was starting to get dark and there were just a few of the children yet to leave. Selma and I were usually the first ones to have our names called out to go home. I did not like being one of the lingering ones wondering if anyone was coming to get you or just leave you there. You know what happens when you are the last ones to be picked up? Phone calls with adults whispering so you cannot hear them saying, "These children are still here, and we need someone to come and get them." Who knows who they are calling? It could be the police or a local government child agency that takes forgotten little children somewhere but not home.

Finally, headlights, and my mom's face at the door apologizing. Who cared? She was there to take us home we would not have to ride in a strange car with police trying to entertain us by turning on the lights or siren, scaring us more than helping.

It was dark out when we pulled into the graveled driveway of the little house with creepy shed and creepier barn. Sis and I still were wearing our coats, hats, and mittens. The wind caused a sting to our bare little faces. Mom got us out of the car, up the stairs and finally in the house only to discover there was no heat. How she knew that the pilot light was out is beyond me, but she did. Under the house with spider webs and damp dirt floor and heaven only knows what she could not see without the flashlight (probably a good thing), she found wherever the flame was out and relit it. It took a while for the house to warm up. It was best to keep our coats and apparatus on until the chill was gone.

It was also Mom who was there when we were sick. She would be taking our temperature, giving us medicine, putting a washcloth on our heads, putting one or both in the tub and changing the sheets if we could not make it to the bathroom— it was all mom.

One night, concerned about a stubborn fever with both of her two young girls, she whisked us off to the emergency room. She was informed we had the flu and given prescriptions to have filled along with instructions for care. For days she and our Great Aunt kept watch over us, encouraging sips of fluids and soup until we were well again.

Inga took care of all these matters. I never heard her complain about Dad not being there. I did not see her sobbing or staying in the bed all day being sad. She carried on and took care of the place we lived and of her two girls. It is not easy being a military wife. Most do not realize and then build up resentment. Being married means sharing these daily struggles. Sharing any struggles with someone that is out protecting the *all* is lonely. It is a challenge that proves too much for most, especially if they do not have a strong support from others experiencing the same obstacles. Many give up and go home to their family leaving the one serving the *all*, alone.

Bobby returned to North Carolina after a deployment sporting a mustache. I recall he may have caught a ride with Santa because the date of arrival was so close to Christmas day. The gifts were abundant with a talking baby doll for me. Selma was given a stuffed monkey holding a banana that if you pulled the string on its side, it made monkey sounds. A fire engine push car and a blue convertible push car were left in the car shed a day earlier because Santa needed to unload early. There were more dolls as tall, if not taller than Selma or me, both dressed in costumes sitting at the tree.

Dad brought a friend by the name of Swede. He was tall with dark hair and very strong. He picked Selma up in one arm and me in the other. I am not sure of his homeland, but he did have an accent. The best guess would be Sweden given the name Swede. I have heard people called the name of Tex, for example, yet they were not from Texas. They just wore an old cowboy hat all the time.

This man was so nice. He brought barbie doll beds so very neatly wrapped with bows included to my dad's girls. Swede said he had heard my dad talk about us and Dad had shown him pictures of his pretty girls. He added he was so happy to meet both of us. His voice was so pleasant. Mr. Swede's eyes seemed to be bright and wide. When he smiled, we could see most of his big, white teeth. He was as exuberant to give us presents, as we were to open them. The beds for our Barbie dolls were as fancy as I have ever seen a toy or an actual bed. The regal headboards topped with red satin bedspreads trimmed in white fringe. A red satin pillow completed the set. We were so thrilled! Mr. Swede was caught up in the excitement. He bent down and scooped us both up again. All three of us were laughing. Selma and I were yelping at dad and mom to look at us. What a fun man.

Although, I did not ever see him again. Dad received letters and a photo of him shirtless with his arms stretched out, a python lying across the back of his neck and wrapped around his muscled, large arms. His shirt hung off his weapon. The gun, huge and black, looking like it could launch a rocket was nearby leaning against a jeep. The stories about his service were legendary. I overheard Dad once tell his racing buddies how many tours Mr. Swede had spent in Vietnam. The man was indeed a very skilled soldier.

I am not sure how our dad accompanied by Mr. Swede arrived to the Christmas visit in North Carolina. It may have been by car. It could have been an airplane into a US city then a bus to get them closer, where someone picked them up. I can guarantee if my grandmother or Aunt Carolyn went along for the ride to pick them up, Dad got an ear full about the purchase of, "The Stove." My dad would not have wanted to debate the purchase of a stove, used to cook food for his children with anyone, including his own mother.

The trouble of that stove may not have even been an issue if my sister would have been named for my grandmother using her first name Abigail or her middle name Margaret or at least her nickname, Babe. I am sure Selma may have acquiesced to that moniker but dad, not at all.

Inga announced when we readied to move to military housing in North Charleston, she had the stove taken over to my grandmother's. I doubt Aunt Inez relished further arguments regarding the matter, wishing all to "Hush now."

Dad's sister, Carolyn, ended up with the stove placed in the same house as she and Uncle Bill moved in not long after we moved out.

* * *

What Base Next?

O ur family had lived mostly in Navy housing since my sister and I were born, although the location varied. I started school when we were stationed in Annapolis, Maryland. We lived in base housing where "Reveille" was played every morning when Old Glory was raised, and "Taps" played every evening when it was lowered. All children stopped playing, stood at attention when "Taps" played. The National Anthem would be played on the screen prior to the start of a movie on base. Everyone, children included, instinctively knew to stand for the anthem. The action was a very well taught reflex.

We, the children, did not comprehend the sacrifice many had offered but we knew it was an expected behavior born out of respect for the military we felt that we too were a part of.

It seemed like those were good times in our family. We had dance night every Friday night in our living room. My daddy had made two large speakers and painted them red. The country music could be heard loud and clear— Red Sovine, Roy Clark and others.

During other times my sister and I would dance in our room to the records our grandfather had bought us. They were mostly from the big band era. The Benny Goodman band and Glen Miller were our starters in music. It was so much fun.

I could not wait to grow up and go to places like the ones I had seen on television. Supper clubs with several circular tables dressed in linen tablecloths and a lit candle. Large, upholstered booths lined the walls with the same type of circular tables with the ensemble sitting on a stage placed at the front of the club encouraging people to take to the dance floor.

There were women dressed up in flowing dresses adorned in accessories brightly glittering when caught by the light. The men dressed up in suits with handkerchiefs always ready if needed. The sharply dressed staff willing to take care of your needs. There would be a coat check booth to leave your coats and wraps to the side of the maître d' station, and an attendant to assist you when you went to powder your nose.

Yes, I really thought that was what adults did when they hired babysitters and went out for an evening of fun! I did watch a lot of Lawrence Welk when I stayed with Aunt Inez. Not to forget, I did view such described set ups at The Chiefs Club on the navy bases. A stage in place with microphone and ready for the adult hours that were past my bedtime even on the weekends.

Daddy made the rank of chief while stationed in Annapolis. He proudly walked us in, The Chiefs Club for dinner on a few occasions. Selma and I ordered Shirley Temples for the first time. It was very exciting. I could not help but smile. The lights were low and music was always playing. I remember hearing Bobby Goldsboro singing his song, "Honey," each time we were present. It was not live music but a jukebox playing during the family hours.

When the snow came it was deep—truly up to my hips deep. It may have been normal to those that lived there but Sis and I had never seen snow. We were unprepared (no snow boots), so mom placed plastic bread bags over our canvas tennis shoes. We did not want to come in, for we were fascinated with making snowballs to throw at one another and other kids.

There was one boy, you know, in every group there seems to always be a bully. This boy had a short crew cut and a head that was like a block that seemed to sit on top of him without a neck. He was always chasing my sister and I or we were always running from him. You know the chicken or the egg dilemma. When he threw a snowball, he hit us every time. He would laugh and throw another.

We escaped him when mom called us in to go buy us some snow boots. When we got to the shoe store my feet were so cold and red. I took my shoes off. My toes were stinging. I sat there and looked at my toes. I was scared my second and third toes had frozen together. Panicked, I called out for my mom, but she assured me my toes had not frozen together. She bought the boots had fur in them and soon warmed my toes and they stopped stinging and itching.

Selma and I were as excited about the snow as much as my dad was not. He reminded us to watch our little, blonde, Pekingese dog when he went out because he would disappear into the snow because of his coloring. I believe that is the main reason dad was outside with a wide silver shovel heaving snow off the sidewalk although he would not admit it. The only reason we were allowed to have the adorable little doggie was our grandfather. Dad's dad is the one that brought the dog as a gift to Selma and me.

The truth was the dog was my mother's dog. She took care of him and loved on him all the time. He loved to eat left over spaghetti—just licked it up out of his plate. It was funny to watch him or hear him with that flattened nose he sounded like a train chugging and slurping the noodles.

Selma showed me where the doggie biscuits were in the closet at the back door. She said they were good and offered me to try one. I looked at it, smelled it and just could not take a bite. Sis shrugged her shoulders and chomped down on the one she held in her hand. I guess she was adventurous from the get-go.

Annapolis is the place where we both began school at Rolling Knowles Elementary. It is the only school I remember participating in a May Pole dance. Of course, I wore pink and green dresses and when my sister began school, she wore blue.

Both mom and dad took interest in our scholastic progress. My sister partici-pated in any homework I was assigned. Dad had us drawing circles within the two solid blue lines in our primary notebook. My sister was tested three times due to her results being off the charts. I wondered if the reason she was claimed to be such a child genius was that she had learned some of the skills from my assignments and the practice dad required. Her brain continued to be awesome because she never needed to take a book home and posted the top grades available. So much for the theory of learning through repetition. Her brilliance could not be denied.

She and I learned to swim while residing on base. The pool was very near the housing units, making it easy to make the early morning swimming lessons. The water was cold so early in the morning. We were shivering but hopped right on in the pool without complaint.

I was five and six years old while Dad was stationed in Annapolis. I remember him bringing home a bicycle he found at the dump. He took it apart, sanded it, painted it red and added the training wheels. The bike was a gift to me from my daddy. He taught me how to ride it. The training wheels came off before we left Annapolis. I rode that little red bike for a few years. I fell off it quite a bit as well. Scrapes on my palms and my knees were ever present.

Dad searched and found a blue bicycle to rehab for Sis. It was fun to have someone to ride with and the bikes made it easier to ride away from the bully boy.

My mom took advantage of whatever area we resided in at the time. Living in Annapolis, Maryland, she took me to many of the landmarks, Grant's Tomb, statue of the soldiers at Iwo Jima, Mount Vernon, and the Tomb of the Unknown Soldier. Oh, how I loved going to the

Smithsonian Museums! My favorite exhibition was the red shoes worn by Judy Garland in the Wizard of Oz. There was something about those sparkling red shoes with a bow, sitting so close to me. I was mesmerized simply staring at them. I truly loved those shoes but at the age of six, I will admit I was too frightened of the movie's flying monkeys to watch the whole movie.

My sister stayed with a sitter I guess because she was too young to be interested in the historical things around us. She sure did miss a lot of cool things. Once mom and I walked to Fords Theatre, the place where Abraham Lincoln was shot by John Wilkes Booth. The poor man was watching a play from the balcony and was shot in the head. The offender, an actor and southern sympathizer, jumped from the balcony ironically snagging his boot on the flag, to land on the stage and break his leg.

Despite the very dramatic tale of true events occurring to one of the nation's finest presidents, I was focused on something else. The theatre seats were so very small, all of them. I could not imagine the people I knew, except for children, being able to sit in them. The tour guide explained the people were so much smaller adding however that President Lincoln was quite tall at six foot four inches in height.

The sight that I will never forget is of a navy wedding with the navy men standing in full dress uniforms, drawn swords held high and crossed for the married couple to exit the church through the tunnel created. It was a cool spring day. A nearby tree's white blossoms gently floated by on a soft breeze as if it were thrown by well-wishers. What a scene to spark fanciful wishes in my little girl head.

Although it was mom and I viewing much of the nation's history, it would be the entire family visiting the zoo frequently. I remember what fun it was to have dad with us. This was long before him sitting with arms crossed and puffed up like a blow fish. He would ask Sis and I which animal our favorite was to visit. He would escort us hand in hand to our chosen animal's staging area. Dad would sweep one of us up in his strong, muscular arms holding on firmly just so we could see past other people. While he held each of us, he would ask us what it was that we liked about that animal, asking us to point out certain characteristics. Dad and I both favored the polar bears. I liked the color of their fur, so thick and white, offset by their black noses and paw pads. The manner in how they would slide into the pool, made just for them, had me giggling. What endeared them to me was how they shook off after climbing out. This huge animal that could eat me in one bite looked silly and fun when they plopped on their bellies extending their back paws upward for all to see. It looked like they did not have a care in the world.

It was so much fun. If you can remember the excitement of when you were a child going somewhere, you know the jitteriness of, "I can't wait to get there" spinning around in your insides. It is as if butterflies are fluttering in your tummy attempting to get you there faster, but no one understands how they should hurry up. It was truly a magical time in our family and all of us were there.

One time, dad came up with a scheme to make a little extra money with a couple of his navy buddies. They drove a truck to Pageland, South Carolina (the watermelon capitol of the world). It was loaded up with watermelons and they brought them back to sell in Annapolis. The talk on the ride was probably full of excitement about what each one of them planned to do with the quick profit.

My dad was driving. He knew the way and knew all the short cuts. I bet he scooted up close in the seat leaning over the steering wheel, his left arm on the wheel and looking at the guys seated on the bench seat. His crystal blue eyes widened when he was interested in the subject. My dad had a way of talking that drew folks in to listen. Believe me, it was not monotone. No doubt, he held up his end of a conversation.

The truck was parked close to the Chief's Club hoping to get the best sales. Some of the melons were cut open to show the bright red melon promising a satisfying sweet taste. What I gathered is the melons did not sell as fast as needed for the summertime heat. An invitation went out to the neighborhood to gather at 17:00, (5 p.m.) for the Watermelon Bust. Yep, exactly as suggested, the melons would be broken up by breaking them open and taking the pieces by hand to eat. This event had a sizeable crowd, and all the melons were eaten so Dad and friends did not need to dispose of them. Dad mentioned that the watermelon business was a bust too!

Family life also had a tainted side. Our parents had gone out one evening and we were asleep well before they arrived home. I heard yelling. Selma heard it too because she sat straight up in her bed. It was a few feet from me. It was scary.

We had never heard our parents yelling at each other. Neither one of us knew what was happening. Selma and I did not get up to go look out our door. We whispered it might not be mom and dad. I think it was Selma that said, "It could be next door?" The yelling soon stopped so we went back to sleep.

We got up the next morning and readied ourselves for school. We always got ready upstairs before going downstairs for breakfast. Mom was usually downstairs in the kitchen. That particular morning, she met us at the landing at the top of the stairs with her yellow, quilted robe on. She started down the steps, and I followed as Selma fixed her shoe then fell in behind me. Mom was a few steps ahead of us. The tie to her robe was not around her waist so it floated up. I pointed toward her for Selma to see what I had seen. Her robe lifted and she did not have any clothes on under her robe. What was worse—our mom had belt marks across her back side. Bright red, belt marks—three of them.

Sis and I did not ask any questions. How do you say to your mom, "Hey, how did you get those belt marks across your behind, mom?" I do not think Sis or I ate anything that morning. We did not go to school that morning. I sure wish we had because we heard way too much adult stuff and of course we had to sit still and be quiet. Mom was on the phone and she started to cry. She told us to stay downstairs until she got ready. "Ready for what?" we asked each other. How did we know any possible answers to that question?

Mom came back downstairs in a dress and slipped on her low heel shoes. She told us to put our bookbags down and come with her. We did as she said and followed her out the door, across the complex and into another unit. Mom had sunglasses on which was odd because it was so early in the morning and the sun was not shining. It was cloudy.

Mom knocked on the door and then stood back a few steps waiting for someone to answer. I had never been here to this unit, so I did not know what was going on at all. Selma and I looked at each other, shrugging our shoulders. It did not take long until an older man opened the door and invited us all in. He asked us to sit on the couch as he and Mom would go to the kitchen to talk a little while.

We two young girls should have been seated in school or a couch somewhere else where we could not hear the entire conversation. The highlights were that mom had drunk too much and was talking to a man of color which led to dancing with the same man. Evidently, my father was very upset and felt mom had become heated and dad had hit her with a belt. Mom was crying. The man was soft spoken asking questions to have a clear understanding of the ordeal.

Selma had flopped back, no longer sitting up straight with legs dangling over the side of the couch. She was swinging her legs and started singing some silly song. I guess she was bored or like me, she did not want to hear any more of mom and dad's business. I told her to sit up and she just shook her whole head while sticking out her tongue with her feet kicking faster.

Perhaps, her perfect brain was exercising ESP for what would be heard next coming from the table in the next room. Mom's voice was louder and then she burst into tears. The man said things to calm her in his soft tone and to understand what it was she had just said. It took a few minutes until the loud hysterics quieted to sniffles mixed with apologies. He went on to say, "It was all right. I am wanting to make sure I heard what you said so I can help you." The tears with the inaudible message were lost again. The chaplain took a different approach. "You seem to be having a hard time so let me say what I think you are telling me and you correct me if you need to. How's that?" I could hear her utter, "Hmmm hmmm." I thought she was nodding her head in agreement before she blew her nose in her hanky.

Selma had stopped swinging her legs and singing her silly words. Her posture was still flopped back but her ears were as perked up as mine. The man mustered up to understand this very upset woman whose accent made the challenge a bit more difficult. He pushed on. "As I understand, what you are saying is that your husband is going to leave you." Mom started to cry again. Yet, the man continued, "And he told you he was not going to come back to your home." Almost screaming she responded, "Thaaat's right." Selma sprung up, scooted close to me and whispered, "Did you hear that?" I just nodded my head.

The lady who lived in the house, Mrs. Chaplain came around the corner with a plate of cookies. She handed us each a napkin and asked if we would like a cookie while the chaplain talked to our mom.

We were both staring in front of us unable to acknowledge the lady. She tilted her head, "I'll just sit the plate right here on the table if you would like one, you can have one." Then as if reading my mind, she said, "It is ok to eat in here. The chaplain and I do all the time." She smiled, turned around and left us sitting there.

We sat and sat. Soon the lady appeared again and had us come into the kitchen. We walked past mom and the chaplain. He was on the phone with mom intently listening to whatever he was saying. She reached out her hand as we walked by as if to stay connected. The lady had a small table set up with small plates with little sandwiches and tiny cups and saucers. She said she often had fairies come by to eat her special made lunches including the bitty bite cakes. If we ate our lunch, she may find some to give us. There was nice, happy music playing low. It was a nice thing she did to help two little girls concern themselves with tiny cupcakes and fairies.

It was a long day attempting to be quiet and smile while listening to adults whispering. Sis and I could not talk to one another without immediate attention from the adults in the apartment. There were a few phones calls placed by the chaplain. Then before dinner the chaplain told my mother, "Bob has agreed to come home after work to talk to you." Sis and I started to gather our things until we heard, "The girls can stay here while you speak. They will be fine. No, not any trouble at all."

Oh yay! We are staying longer. I was ready to go home, take a bath and go to bed. Who cares if it is four o'clock in the afternoon? Thank heavens, Mrs. Chaplain turned on the television set. We could sit there and forget about parents yelling, hitting, and if we were going to have a place to live.

MY MOTHER'S SUITCASE

We had watched a couple of shows. The news had not come on when mom came back to pick us up. I was so thankful she let us run on home. She stayed to update the chaplain on the meeting. As grateful as I was to go home, I was more so that my daddy was home.

Sis was in her pajamas before I happened to get mine from the dresser. We were exhausted. Yes, we wanted to go to bed. We were almost always in bed before Walter Cronkite with the CBS Evening News was on at the scheduled time slot of seven p.m. My mother insisted we were not only in bed but also quiet by the time he made his appearance in our living room every evening. It did not matter if it was summer and the sun still shining—we had to go to bed. It did not matter through our open windows (due to no air conditioning in housing at that time), we could hear other kids playing outside—we had to go to bed. We were like little babies tucked away so mom could visit with the anchor man and the other reporters.

Rarely, was this rule bent. Occasionally, permission may have been granted if we had taken a nap to view a special show like the Wizard of Oz. Allowing one of the girls to be awake past seven p.m. may be considered as a reward for a good grade. The night after the day spent with the chaplain was not an evening either of us wanted to be awake or giggling.

It was a few weeks later when Mayflower pulled up to our door on Eucalyptus Street. They packed up the truck and took all our belongings to storage apart from what we had in our suitcases. The suitcases were packed in the trunk like they were presents to be unwrapped upon arrival at our destination.

***

To North then South Carolina

We spent several weeks in Concord, North Carolina. This time our hosts were my dad's Uncle Buc and Aunt Linney. This was on the Lefler side (my dad's father's brother). They resided in a cotton mill community and walked to work on third shift just a few blocks from their house. My mom walked Selma and I to a nearby elementary school. We attended for six weeks.

My mother, sister and I shared a very large bedroom. I clearly remember the braided rug for its colors were yellow, green, and brown. Selma and I both were sick, seems we always did the flu, chicken pox, mumps and whatever virus was going around—together. There was vomiting, fever and a trip to the emergency room again. That rug with the circular pattern, the colors crisscrossing did not help with the waves of nausea. The retching continued into a perfectly placed bucket beside the bed. It seemed we were only sick when we were in North Carolina. Perhaps sick of being in transition led to a decreased immune system.

Dad returned from being out at sea. He received orders to a new duty station in Charleston, South Carolina. It was 1968 and I would finish second grade at Dorchester Elementary School.

There would be no worry of frozen toes or losing our dog in the snow. Charleston would be the longest duration of any base for our family of four plus a blond, Pekingese. The housing complex was off base bordering the marsh and waters of the Ashley River. We were in the row closest to the marsh on an end unit. I could see the radar lights blink on and off at night out of my bedroom window. It was hypnotic counting the blinks as I drifted off to sleep.

There were families moving out and in all the time. Moving meant moving boxes and the purging of stuff. The boxes could be flattened to ride down the graded slopes in front of a line of units. The stuff left behind was like finding a pirate's treasure.

Once there was an old camera, so we played Hollywood, taking pictures without film for days on end. Another family tossed out a long ponytail, like a wig, and we used it like it was a tail on a horse, placing it in the back waistband of our pants. One time I did not have to dig in the boxes for one of the mom's knew how much I liked to play dress up and gave me a few fancy dresses, skirts, a pair of high heels, a purse, some jewelry, and a pair of sunglasses. I posed for a camera with film with a skirt pulled up to be a dress, standing in high heels and even had the long gloves. Oh, the purse was tucked under one of my arms. I looked like I was headed to a night out dancing. I knew I was destined to be a star in Hollywood! My mother had told me, in America you can be anything you want to be when you grow up. At that time with those dress up clothes, I wanted to be Mitzi Gaynor in South Pacific singing, "Wash that man right out of my hair." It would have to be put on hold for a few years at least, until I could hold up a bodice on a dress. Until then I would search more boxes in the back of housing for tossed out magic wands turning hair pieces into horse tails and clothing magically stirring a little girl's imagination to the stage.

More fun could be had at the playground at the end of our road. It was equipped with a merry-go-round, monkey bars, swings and a slide that would scorch your behind on the sunny days. Large oak trees stretched out long limbs which kept the playground shady most of the time. The afternoon sun rays would sneak under the limbs and hit the metal slide. If you were not thinking and took the metal gripped spiked steps up, lowered your bottom to a sitting position then you risked a scorched bottom or thighs or both. You could sense heat within seconds of the descend. Placing your tennis shoes flat down in front you put the brakes on so you could haul over the side to stop the torment.

It was safe to ride your bike all around the complex. There were two small ponds with streams feeding into one. Some of us spent hours catching minnows in jars then letting them go and trying all over the next day. A field located near one of the ponds was large enough to play games like red rover, tag, mother-may-I, or hide-and-go-seek. It was always more fun when there are a lot of other children to play games.

There was still plenty of time for my sister and I to play together. We found a pipeline close to the playground. It stretched out through the marsh to the Ashley River. We walked the pipe until it came to a spot where only the plough mud could be seen. It was at least a ten-to-twelve-foot drop. Selma kept on walking until she reached the other side. She quizzically looked back, "Why are you not coming?" I flat out told her I was too scared that I may fall. She laughed and kept on walking.

I sat down on the pipe, placed my hands together in front of me and scooted across the section with the large drop. The pipe was hot from the sun beaming down on it. I moved quickly so not to scorch my legs. At least I was not focusing on toppling off into the plough mud below. Selma was just beyond my view waiting on me. I caught up to where she was waiting. She called me a scaredy cat. We took verbal jabs at each other as we continued to walk, stopping when we caught a glimpse of a honeysuckle vine. The marsh grass had made a shadow across that stretch. The metal we were walking on was not hot, so we straddled the pipe letting our flip-flopped feet swing on either side, picking off the sweet flowers, trying to catch the honey on our tongues.

Faintly, we could hear music. It could not be anyone's radio from housing. We were too far out even if there was a car radio on at the playground. The sounds were similar to when mom took us to the symphony and the instruments were warming up, each member of the orchestra playing their own instrument from a different section of the various selections on the program. It could be quite loud, not in sync at all, sort of a sound you may hear from a Dr. Seuss quizzical band.

The marshland music began to take form, playing together so Sis and I could hear the sound much better. We had fun sitting there on the pipeline listening to a concert. Selma and I would return many times, some of the times together.

There were times I went out myself with nothing but the low country marsh grasses and water surrounding me, listening to the music and humming along. Other days I nestled among the low-lying limbs of the oak back behind the monkey bars, softly singing some tunes I strung together with a few words that seemed to fit. It was a charmed time.

After several rides in the back seat of the GTO during Mother's errands, observing in either direction of housing, Sis and I took a guess at the location of the marsh music at navy housing was on Azalea Drive banked by the Ashley River. The final resting place for many locals was located on the east (a peaceful cemetery with huge live oak trees provided much shade for the bereaved). A maze of sandy roads leading to the only entrance also served as the exit with a concrete arch holding swinging gates that were padlocked with a heavy chain and lock after hours. I had walked through there a time or two.

The land close to the marsh did not host any graves. It was evidently a place that some liked to go and hit golf balls for there were a litter of white dimpled balls in that area. You could see some of the balls stuck out in the marsh grass. Some of the boys in housing would scramble over to collect the balls. I felt like an intruder the couple of times I crossed the fence over to the sanctuary. All I did was walk around being ever-so-careful not to step on top of any of the resting places of someone's relative. I saw a man hitting golf balls once and although he was not near any of the grave sites. I felt the act was disrespectful. I doubt he would have liked anyone staging a funeral on a golf course when he paid to play.

The marsh spread west between navy housing and The Jenkins Orphanage. It was the residents of the orphanage we heard playing the music. Little did we know the history of the once infamous band (a band that was requested to play for the Queen of England). The band members from there had started a dance craze that swept the land and was named for the city where it was first performed, Charleston. Matter of fact, requests for the band to appear encouraged the organizing of three bands formed from residents of the orphanage.

The Jenkins Orphanage Band were credited as a part of the early days of jazz, all due to a pastor who saw a need to provide a home for many young boys who wondered around with no place to call home. His goal was to have the boys learn a trade thereby preparing them to support themselves when they left the orphanage.

Selma and I liked to go to the marsh behind the units. There were spaces in the plough mud that had holes, some that bubbled. Fiddler crabs popping in and out of these holes provided much entertainment. The male crabs with large claws were of particular interest to the daring Selma. She would get a marsh grass pointing at the crab's large claw hoping it would grab it. The grass became shorter, and her hand became closer to the claws of the fiddler crab. It did not take long until she would just reach down and pick up the crab by its large claw. Of course, she would extend her arm out and offer for me to hold it. She would creep closer and closer. I would then take off and run while she laughed saying, "Come on, it won't hurt you."

* * *

Dancing the Marsh Fire

Mom had arranged for me to continue dance classes once we had settled in Charleston. Ms. Simmons conducted dance classes at a Park Circle Community Center close to the navy base. Mom enrolled me in tap, ballet, jazz and baton. My sister had tried dance at another studio. The battle of making her to get in the car to go to class became too much for mom so she took her out. Selma did not go to her own dance class, so going to mine and waiting out in the community center was not a pleasurable experience for my mother.

One afternoon Selma begged to stay at home. One of our friends said she checked with her mom, and it was all right for Selma to stay with them until we got back home. Mom was ok with not arguing with Selma for the next hour and a half, so she agreed.

Mom took me to dance, we came home and noticed a fire truck behind the housing units. They soon wrapped up what they were busy with and headed out.

It was later that evening when we were lying down for bed that my sister began to cry. She did not cry hardly ever. I called out for mom, and she quickly came into our room. Mom sat on my sister's bed and spoke to her while she was crying. Selma told her she was crying because she saw the horse die on the TV that night. Mom, attempting to console her, led to me being requested to leave the room. Fine with me. I went downstairs with dad and watched television. Mom soon came downstairs informing dad, not the dying horse story. I listened intently as Mom relayed what had happened when she had taken me to dance class that afternoon. Selma and Stacey decided to play in the marsh out behind our unit. They had made a tunnel through the marsh grass. One of the girls had matches so they took turns striking them trying to get a reed to catch a light. A reed did catch and so did the marsh. A neighbor noticed the fire and called the fire department.

Dad was upset mentioning how the units could have caught fire. He did not forget to add there was a gas line nearby. He looked up and saw my face and instructed me to go to bed. Selma was calm and I honestly did not know what to say to her. I got into bed and locked onto the blinking light outside the window. It took counting many more blinks than usual before drifting off to sleep that night.

The next morning at the breakfast table mom told us of her plan to arrange a tour of the fire station. It was the station nearest the housing so no doubt it was the fireman that answered the call to the marsh being aflame. It did take a couple of days to arrange but the day soon arrived. My mom loaded up the car with the two fire bugs, Selma and friend Stacey and guess who also was to tag along on the field trip—me. The one time I did not want to sit in the front seat, there I was perched up front for all to see. My sister and her partner in crime were piled up in the back seat, so excited to be together. They were smiling and chatting.

It was a quick drive down Azalea Drive to where it intersected with Leeds Avenue. The fire department sat across from the stoplight. My mother pulled in slowly and parked in the front. I got out and held the seat up for the two buddies to exit out of the car. I followed behind them happily to be in the back as mother greeted the fireman at the door.

We were taken for a tour around the fire station and even had the opportunity to sit in the driver's seat of the fire truck. Once the tour was completed the sermon about the importance of fire safety commenced. The wrap-up was the statistics of injuries and deaths occurring every year from carelessly started fires. All three of us were given a coloring book with the facts taught during our visit and pledged to help the fireman by preventing fires.

MY MOTHER'S SUITCASE

Mom packed us all back in the car, but we did not head in the direction of home. She told us there was another place she wanted to take us. The car turned left on Leeds taking a right at the next stop light onto Dorchester Road. She took the road behind the library, and I thought if she asks me, the me that did not strike a match—the me that was nowhere around the smoking marsh grasses—to do a Smoky the Bear book report about preventing forest fires, well I had to take my non-smoldering ground and say—no ma'am.

Mom did not turn right to the library parking lot. No, she went on a few feet further down the road and turned into the parking lot of the police station. Yes, she did. Hold on a minute, I would prefer to—be honored to—present a book report rather than go in the police station. I looked back at my sister, and she just shrugged her shoulders. I squinted at her so she would know I was mad at her and her friend, the fire starters! Mom was jubilant as she held up the seat for Selma and Stacey to climb out of the back seat. In an act of, "OK, this is where I draw the line" or "Do not think I earned the privilege to go in there," I sat still in the front seat. The front passenger door was not opened. I sat with my hands folded in my lap looking down at my hands. Mom ducked her head into the car to grab her purse and said, "Ok, we are here. It is time for you to get out. Go ahead and open the door. Hurry up now." I looked up at her with my seat belt still buckled and in a quiet voice said, "If it's all right with you mama, I will just wait in the car for ya'll. I will lock the door. You do not have to worry about me. If you would prefer it, I will go over to the library and wait until you have completed your tour." Mother looked at me as a sweet mother from the south would (but of course she was from another country), yet still she had perfected the veiled threat to an art form as many women from the south had done for a couple hundred plus years. She said to me, getting closer and quieter as she approached, "Now darling, what kind of mother would I be if I left you in this sizzling hot car or to wander to and through the library all by yourself?" I started to say, a perfectly wonderful kind of mother that would not punish one sister for the sins of the other one. My mother shushed me and told me not to fret my pretty little head and come join her as we all walked up the concrete steps, opened the doors to step inside of the police station.

This was not a happy time and certainly not a happy place. My mother left us three girls standing as she walked over to the officer at the desk. There were a couple of benches, but we were not going to sit down on them. One man was lying down on one with his mouth open and every little bit he would raise his arms and swat at something around him with his eyes still closed. The other bench had a woman sitting and facing the side. She was quietly talking as if someone was sitting next to her but although she could not see the person was not there. We sure did see no one was sitting beside her. Every few minutes she would reach down beside her and stroke the air and make baby talk.

We three girls scooted closer together and held hands as if we thought we were going to be separated. I looked at my sister and said, "I shouldn't even be in here in this place." She just shrugged her shoulders as a man coming in the door bumped into her. I guess he was not used to looking for kids inside a bad people place. He smiled and apologized as he squeezed by us. Mom had come back to join our little group. I wonder if she thought this was fun. This certainly was not the type of sightseeing I was used to with her as a guide. No, this one is in the thumbs-down category from me.

Mom said to us, huddled in a tight circle, "It won't be long now. It is good I called ahead, or they may not have seen us." I was about to ask to see us for what? when a police officer came to our tight little group and addressed my mom. He pointed to a door over to the far right. It was past the woman talking to herself on the bench and the man at the desk, more behind him and in the corner. We followed the officer with my mom in the front. We held onto one another's clothes. I suppose we looked like baby ducks following the mama duck toward the water for our first swim. There were so many people coming in and out of doors or from behind desks.

We were about to reach the corner door when the one next to it flew open as if a wild wind had pushed it open. Out stepped a man with a short sleeve plaid shirt with torn up hems on the sleeves. His hair was dark and oily looking. What I noticed first was that his hands and feet had cuffs on them, so he shuffled his feet to walk. He was looking around the room like a hurt animal, you know when they are looking for a way from your care. My guess is that he would have liked to escape from the police officer holding onto his handcuffs. He looked down at the three of us girls and I swear I heard him growl! I know Selma and Stacey heard him too because we all did a little yelp and pushed forward to get away from him. We made

Mom run into the officer in front of her. Mother snatched her head around to stare a hole through us and to mouth for us to behave.

The officer opened the door and pointed to an empty bench where we could be seated to wait for another officer to come along and take us wherever we were destined to be. My mother was the only one whose feet could touch the floor from the wooden bench, so we all swung our feet. We were on the verge of a good routine when a woman came over and told us the officer of the day was ready to talk to us now. She walked us down yet another hallway. It felt like we fell into some sort of maze. My hope was of the possibility that if there was an exit, we may be led to some underground tunnel from the civil war days and we would pop up at Magnolia plantation. Nah, that will not happen.

It was clear the officer approaching us was going to talk to mom so maybe we could be patted on the head and told to be good little girls then sent on our merry little way. That did not happen. We were introduced and much to my dismay, I was not distinguished from the two firebugs. The officer took us through the process when someone was going to be charged with some type of wrongdoing.

They let us see the fingerprinting area and the place they took their photos. Selma asked if they would take her photo, but the officer replied if they did, they would have to explain why they were booking a little girl. The photos are numbered, and each has its own copy. It would be chaos trying to explain how a little girl's photo was on the photo strip. Selma and Stacey had caused enough chaos as far as I was concerned.

The officer spoke of how most people ended up there. It was a string of bad choices and often they did not get caught until one day after so many bad choices the police found them out. They were then brought into places all over the city like this, processed before going to see the judge, or wait in a bigger place to see the judge. He was slowly walking toward a jail cell. It had bars from floor to ceiling. There were no windows. It did have a couple of cots anchored to the block wall. Against one wall there was a sink, no mirror, and a toilet without a toilet seat—all right there in the open with no curtains and no door to shut when someone went to the potty. The first question we all asked when he completed his tour was about the toilet with no seat and no door. We were told people will get angry sometimes when they are locked up. They all want to go home. When they determine it is going to be a while before they can go home or anywhere else other than that boring cell, they will sometimes tear up anything to hurt someone (or themselves) to get out. So, the reason for no toilet seat is it can be removed and used as a weapon. The prisoners must be monitored at all times so if they need to relieve themselves, they will have to use the facilities provided.

The police encouraged each of us to make good choices so we would not end up in a place like it. We agreed as we walked out to the car that we were going to stay out of trouble. We sure did not want to go to the bathroom in front of everybody. No way!

We could not wait to tell dad about the toilet with no seat. He asked my sister if she was going to start any more fires. Selma replied quickly, "No Sir!" Dad looked at me and asked how I liked the day's activities. I shrugged my shoulders. He said, "What, you did not like seeing the toilet with no seat?" I told him, "I was scared." "Scared of what? There were a lot of police around. It was probably the safest place you could be." I added it was smelly. Then of course he wanted to know what it smelled like. "Sort of like dirty clothes inside of a hot dirty car." My daddy asked, "How do you know what that smells like? Don't your daddy keep clean cars and a clean truck for you to ride around in?" I smiled at him and told him, "Daddy, no one keeps a car as clean as you do!" He tickled us both until we were squealing.

Dad not only kept the GTO and his 1966 Ford pick-up truck running in tip top shape, but they also sparkled and shined—all the time. They were both a pale yellow with black details. The GT0, also a 1966, had a black hardtop. He spent a lot of time cleaning and drying them. Looking at him washing one of them you would think he liked it. Not like it was a chore or a task he was required to do, he enjoyed cleaning the vehicles.

One day, I asked him if I could help, maybe he could teach me how to wash the car. When I say he begrudgingly agreed, I mean he responded like a kid playing with his favorite toy and he was told to share it. He mumbled and told me to come on while he pointed out what supplies are required for the truck this time. He let me pour the soap in the bucket and squirt the water that made pretty bubbles. We were off to a good start. He took the hose to rinse off the truck, reached for the cloth in the bucket and started washing the top of the cab while holding the hose in the other hand. He would rinse, wash, rinse and start on another part of the truck. I stood back as it seemed my presence was one—in his way as he maneuvered his way around his beloved truck and, two—annoying him by being there. I jumped straight on, dumping the bucket to rinse and fill again with soap and clean water. I was not ready to rinse out the cloth evidently. He had a process for rinsing the cloth with the hose pipe, stretching the cloth long ways wringing out water and repeating it twice.

I stayed at least five feet away as he made his way around the truck. I did not want to bother him but wanted to be there if he needed something. This was not as much fun as I thought he made it look. He had washed and dried the cab, the body, all the glass and three chrome wheels. Now he was down to the last of the wheels. I do not know why he told me I could get the hose and rinse off the wheel, but I did. I stood next to him squatting beside the wheel and a gust of wind came up from the river. The gust blew some of the water back toward my dad and in his face. Well, he grabbed the nozzle redirecting the water to stop spraying his face. He had that tolerant yet irritated look on his face, shaking his head. He said, "Don't you know not to spray into the wind?" I replied as I started to tear up, "No, daddy." He responded, "It's all right. You can go on in now. Thank you for helping me. I'll get this stuff up." Dropping my head, I dragged myself into the house and up to my room.

＊＊＊

Southern Dirt Track Racing

BOBBY ON RACE DAY

S aying my dad was a motor head would be an understatement. As Aunt Inez had told us, this was evident in his youth. My best guess is that once he became a chief and then a Master Chief Petty Officer, he had more administrative assignments leaving him yearning to mess with grease and tools. I must mention despite his occupation and his hobbies, his fingernails were always clean. I mean, I never saw a bit of grease on his hands or under his nails, ever. No, he did not wear gloves. He used rags to wipe his hands and some goop stuff that he washed his hands with at the end of a job. I do not know what his secret was and to answer any naysayers, yes, I had seen him with his hands inside of an engine. There is a photo of him standing inside a car engine space with tools in hand.

When Bobby began working with race cars, he dressed in the colors of the car on race day. The cars were usually painted the colors of yellow with black and red numbers/trim or white with red and blue. Bobby wore white pants with pressed creases with a yellow, black, red, or blue shirt. He wore coveralls but the white pants always were clean as when he placed them on.

When we moved to Charleston, Dad found a group of like-minded motor heads. The shop was a few miles from navy housing. It was a detached double sized garage at a man's house that not only liked to race cars but fish as well. He and dad were fast friends. He was married and had a daughter, a son and a German shepherd named Champ.

Champ and I liked each other. He was a big dog especially compared to our tiny Pekingese. Champ let me rub my fingers through his coarse hair and scratch his back. I was usually afraid of big dogs, thinking they would bite me, but not Champ. He always had a nice look on his face, never once snarled or growled at me.

The son, Kenneth, was my age and cute, but sharing so much time with our families in the racing environment made us more like cousins than any other type of relationship. The daughter, Rachel, was a year or so older than me but it was Selma and she that formed a tight bond that lasted for several years.

Dad would come home, eat dinner, and rush out to the race car shop. My sister and I could not go with him most of the time because he would arrive home too late on school nights. We did like going because it was fun to be in the shop playing with the heavy jacks by cranking them up and riding them back down. We made friends with the sister and brother, after all we spent a lot of time together. Selma was often in the truck and off before I could say I wanted to go. The times that I voiced I wanted to go before they went; my dad would flip a coin. This did not set well with me. I stopped asking to go and found other things to do with friends living in the neighborhood.

Our entire family of four would go to the races on Saturday nights. Special main events were scheduled for Friday and Saturday nights and usually on holidays like Memorial and Labor Day. The season was early spring to end late in the fall. Dad drove the truck that either pulled the car on a trailer or later a truck specialized with racks that allowed you to drive the car onto the bed of the truck. There was also a rack to place tires. I sat up on the tires to watch "Car 25", in the heat and main races. I cheered "Car 25", until my throat hurt and could barely speak. My mother sat in the cab reading, coming out only for the same races. She stood up on the bed of the truck adorned in team colors.

My sister and I were not allowed to stay in the pit area. We played with kids of other drivers, mechanics and car owners in a fenced-in play pen called the infield. We would chase one another, pick up and stack discarded paper drink cups then stomp on them. Sometimes we would have hot wheel cars and make a track in the dirt.

There was an electrified energy on race day. So much buzz from the time we changed clothes to the racing colors then all loaded up in the truck. We were headed for a 3/8 mile dirt track in a rural area called Knightsville. Despite the location, it was named The Summerville Speedway. The dirt was not local because local dirt was sand, not good for turning a top speed. The track was probably made of trucked in red clay. It was packed tight and provided a hard surface.

I was a prissy girl but there was something about arriving at the track, topping the track itself to ride down across it into the pit area where all the cars would line up in a parked spot. The crew for the car would work on it in that parking spot. If you were a regular, you had staked out a specific parking spot for the car.

We were of course early, which helped to pick up the nuances like the crackling of the speakers playing country music, hearing the heavy chains clunk on the flatbeds, the strain of the wench releasing the tow line easing the car down off the truck bed. The smell of the rubber tires burning thick in the air. Hearing men yelling one syllables as greetings to others making their way into the pit area. The ping of the corn popping in the metal kettle in the small infield concessions that served the pit area as well.

The first thing and strict instruction was to wait for dad to tell us when it was safe to get out of the truck. He did not need to be getting the car off the trailer and worry about one of his daughters getting hit. The car would be unloaded and then we received the all-clear to proceed to the infield. We were to walk alongside the fence line in the pit area to the fenced entry into the infield so we could avoid any other incidents with man or mechanics. Sis and I usually took a good look around to see what cars had arrived to know what kids may be there early like we were. The cutest boy in Wando Woods was also the cutest boy at the racetrack. His dad had the shop at their house across the street from Wando Woods Baptist Church. He would come into the infield some of the time but most of the time, it is my guess, (he was at an age to show interest in the car and all things racing), he was in the pit area with his dad and the racing team.

Being early was a cool thing unless it was summer and a really hot day. There are no trees at the racetrack to block the view, so no shade to stand under. The bathroom could offer a quick break from the sun beating down on your head, but it really was not a place you wanted to hang out in at all. It was best to move your long hair, wet the back of your neck with cool water from the sink, and move on out.

Mom had lunch for us before we left. I did not eat much because I was too excited to eat much at the time. Oh, both mom and dad reminded us to eat because they were not buying stuff from the concession stand because it was too expensive. Adding, just in case we had forgotten all the hundreds of times Selma and I had been told before that no coolers were allowed.

As it goes, after a few hours of playing in the sun, a kid gets hot and thirsty. The hunger sets in when the sun sets, and the heat races are over. The time you are waiting for the main event can be trying if you did not save your allowance money. I would bring my allowance most of the time and spend it at the concession stand. I kept my cup from my drink so I could fill it up from the water cooler on the truck, but kids were prohibited from being in the pit area unless accompanied by a parent. This meant you held out until Mom would meet you at the gate for the heat or main races.

There was a day that was as hot as a penny sitting on the railroad track at noon in the middle of July. Dang hot—sweat eases from your forehead to your temples hot—and that is without moving a muscle. I had spent the dollar I had brought and had gotten water from the cooler. The ice in the cup was long crunched on to quench the thirst.

I went to the fence in front of the truck where I could get Mom's attention while she was reading in the cab. She always was prepared with two or three books in case there was a protest at the end of the race. That meant the car being protested usually won and someone thought they were cheating so they paid to have the protested car engine torn down to reveal what the contenders thought would prove the unfair advantage. It took time to tear down engines and sometimes either before, during or after, tempers would flare, and a fight broke out prolonging the process even more. One book may not have gotten mom through but being prepared with two or three would keep her mind otherwise occupied.

It was not difficult to have mom's eyes perk up to look at you shake the fence. She would place her finger on the spot she was at and then we proceeded to play a game of charades. It was almost impossible to verbally give a message over racing cars on the track. I rubbed my throat, turned my cup upside down to show it was empty and the bottom was busted out. She pointed to me and then at her palm, signing me about the money I brought. I pointed at the cup and rubbed my tummy then chomped my teeth together to let her know I had bought the drink and some crackers. Rubbing my index finger and thumb shrugging my shoulder was a reply that I did not have any more money. She returned the same gesture, indicating she did not have any money either. She mouthed and pointed her thumb over her shoulder for me to, ask your dad. I shook my head, "No." She shook her head, "Yes." After I stomped my right foot while shaking my head no, Mom shrugged her shoulders and returned her eyes to the page she was reading.

Jeez, it had come to this. I had to ask my dad for money. I held a healthy fear of my dad. No, he did not hit me randomly. I only could recall a couple of spankings but that was a long time ago. It is sort of like anyone with good sense when they look at the ocean. It matters not what a good swimmer you are, there is a deep respect for the unpredictability and power of the sea. Now, my sister did not have a fear of anything it seems, including my dad. She would ask him for what she wanted at any time and not be concerned if he would say, "No." Heck, she expected a "Yes", every time. And you know what for her it pretty much was a," Yes", every time.

It took me a while to gather up the courage to even flag him over to the gate close to the concession stand. I had to wait in between heat races then to rattle the fence, have someone notice and they tap my dad's shoulder. He looked back toward the fence and rolled his eyes. His face always spoke volumes without a dial or speaking a word. I pointed to the gate. He walked over as if the world was set on fire, and we were about to fall into the crevice to be burnt to a crisp. He locked his fingers of his left hand in the fence and slightly bent over to hear what I was going to ask of him. I knew not to try his patience by having him ask me more the once what it was that I wanted so I spoke up, competing with the cars returning for their pit stop. "Daddy, I am thirsty. May I have money for a drink?" I asked as confidently as a tiny grain of sand facing the mighty ocean. His eyes widened and looked at me in mine. I showed him my cup. He pointed at the spigot coming out of the side of the concession stand. It was no more than a foot off the ground to keep the race teams from filling up coolers and such. And it was on the pit side of the fence, not to mention how filthy it had to be. I showed him my broken cup again.

The Chief released his hand from the fence, huffed as he reached around to his back pocket for his wallet and gruffly said, "How much is it?" Puffing back out all while, he rolled his eyes so I only could see the white of his eyes before he closed them shut. Meekly clearing my voice, responding with a faint, yet audible, "60 cents." He said, "Fine. Bring me back the change", extending a dollar bill in my direction. I took the dollar and of course replied with a "Thank you, sir." He waved me off as he turned and walked away while placing his wallet back in his back pocket of the white pressed pants.

His change was given to him when we entered the gate for the main event. Selma asked me what that was for, I told her the story. She said, "I never give him the change back and he does not say anything to me. You should have kept it."

The car in the winner's circle would take a lap around the track with the checkered flag. Many times, the kids (there were six of us between the owner/ driver, shop owner/mechanic and my dad), would be allowed to ride sitting in a back window space holding onto a rollbar on the inside with the checkered flag in the other. When it was my turn, I would pick someone else to ride in with me, so I did not feel like I was going to drop the flag or fall out of the window space. My heart was fast paced with the revving of the engine and my breath was hard to catch due to the excitement. I was lightheaded from the rumbling of the power in the engine. It was a few moments when all my senses were on point overload and though it was fun, it almost overwhelmed me. I sighed in relief when dad or someone else would scoop me out and place my feet back on the track.

One of the many fun things of being one of the top racing teams was the winning. I do not mind telling you, it was a much better feeling then blowing an engine and having to come in the pit to watch the finish of a race without your car on the track. Our team won a lot of races, so we were happy quite a bit. Our parents loosened up and we gained perks like walking around on the track, of course after all the cars had cleared the track. I think it took a little while at the pay-out window when you had something to collect.

The celebration continued as we left the track and we all met at the Shoney's on Dorchester Road. Behind the restaurant fence was the house and race car shop so it was not too far to unload the trailer. Shoney's was open late, so our group did not have to rush. We were allowed to order what we wanted which for me was usually a hot fudge sundae. Our group sat together but the adults were at one table and the not-yet adults sat at another table.

After the order was taken, I always excused myself to the restroom. It was cleaner than the racetrack. The lights were brighter so you could see yourself in the mirror. I would wash my hands and then notice how dirty my face was. Wiping a paper towel across my forehead, the towel had red dirt from the dust thrown off by the cars at the track. I was always saying "Yuk", proceeding to wash my entire face to remove the racetrack remnants.

Sundays, the families gathered at the house of the shop. Dad usually washed the race car taking care as he did with his own. The men gathered in the living room to debrief the race and the performance of "Car 25." It was some foreign language that did not keep my attention, so I went outside with the other not yet adults. We would sit in the yard and talk or hang out in the shop listening to the radio.

BOBBY AND CAR 25

Our family and those friends became like a large extended family due to spending all that time together for years. We even traveled to other tracks and car shops, visiting owners and mechanics together during the winter months. These were places further south, so they were still up and running with the warmer weather. The team made friends with Eldon Yarbrough in the state of Florida. He came to Summerville a few times to drive, "Car 25." He did well and liked winning races. His brother, LeeRoy Yarbrough was the first driver to win NASCAR's Triple Crown in 1969. We also met his wife Wanda (with red hair).

LeeRoy had won two Lincoln Continental cars, one white and one black. Wanda drove her white one to the track, parking it in the infield. She and I sat in it while she showed me the electronic buttons for locks and to raise and lower the windows. I was mesmerized when she turned on the air conditioning full blast as we listened to Elvis Presley sing, "Hound Dog." I think she loved listening to him as much as I did because she knew all the words as we sang along with him. I know my dad and his friends were thrilled to meet the brothers Yarbrough— LeeRoy and Eldon—but I do not know if their zeal matched mine in meeting Mrs. Wanda Yarbrough.

Our huge racing family gathered for large cookouts. The first one I remember was held at the race car shop. It took a few days with everyone having different chores. The day of the party, I was so grossed out by being assigned the task with Rachel to pop off the heads and devein shrimp from a wooden barrel (bought fresh from a shrimp boat at Folly Beach). There was other sea life in the barrel beside shrimp. It took me several years to recover enough to eat shrimp again.

The heavy equipment and car had been moved out of the way in the shop area. There was an abundance of food, and someone was handling the music, playing it loud in the shop. Someone had strung up big speakers in four corners of the shop. The floor, usually with oil spots, had been cleaned and dancing was encouraged. It did not take much prodding to have me dance for that was, at the time, the one thing I did well. I danced to Roy Orbison's, *Pretty Woman* and when I was finished, my dad had it played again so my mom could watch. He was amazed. I felt a kind of happy that I did not feel very often where my dad was involved.It was quite wonderful.

We had various menus. A pig was roasted at one event. Fish was served when we gathered at Short Stay (the Navy Recreation Area located on Lake Moultrie). Believe it or not, the largest fish caught that day was with a cane pole by a twelve-year-old me. My daddy was so proud boasting to everyone that I had out fished even him. I was certainly surprised myself to hear the news and I proudly posed with the fish in a picture taken by my mother. My sister had no patience for waiting for a fish to nibble on a line, to make a fluorescent bopper move, and go under the water. She had placed her cane pole down within five minutes heading for the tire swing hanging high in a nearby tree.

The racing family also traveled to race in dad's old stomping grounds, Concord, N.C. All stayed with one of my dad's family or another. In turn many of those relatives traveled to Charleston to watch "Car 25", race at its home track. They spoke about members of our racing family and that shared time, just as the racing family would inquire about members they had stayed with while in North Carolina.

***

The Base has Privileges

There are privileges of being a military brat. The housing area usually had a playground and there were always plenty of kids to hang out and play.

The bases themselves served up quite a few extras and you could only access the base if you were supplied with a sticker, much like an inspection sticker on the driver's side of the lower side of the windshield. A guarded gate at each entrance was usually manned with at least two marine sentries. Your car must slow for the guard to view the sticker then wave you on through the gate. If there was an issue with the sticker (it was expired, or a person did not have one) they were to park to the right of the gate. An office building was located before you passed the gate staffed with military personnel to address problems. All this was to assure only people on the base are the ones allowed on the base. It was not open to the public.

Those who entered the pre-gate office building usually presented their military identification card, much like a driver's license, and the matter could be resolved. A new sticker or a daily pass was given which was presented to the guard. He would wave you on in.

The base had a speed limit lower than what was usually in civilian neighborhoods. The roads where lined with large, chain links painted white and swagged from post to post. The links had to be ones from the ships due to their size being two feet in length and each part of the link having a ten inch or more diameter (not the size of a chain bought for a dog collar!). It was not unusual to see sailors with paintbrushes and buckets out freshening up with more white paint. It seemed everything else on base was painted gray. Those sailors or marines were most likely serving time in the brig that was also on base.

Occasionally, my sister and I would see a small sized pick-up truck going by with ladders and all kind of tools. It was very noticeable due to the model of a large size angry bee with a Navy cap on his head, a hammer, and other tools in his hands. The bee adorned, with tattoos on his arms, was mounted to the top of the cab of the truck. We were informed they were, "The Seabees." The company of sailors with duties to fix things that needed to be fixed and build things that needed to be built. Selma and I weren't concerned with their duties. We just thought the truck was cute. *No offense to any current or veteran Seabee personnel.*

Another sight was a concrete tower standing along the main roadway on base. It was for training the firefighters enlisted in the Navy and Marines. We came upon them more than once fully dressed in firefighting garb during the summer, entering the tower, while pulling long hoses as they went in. Once, smoke was wafting in the sky before the tower was in view. The uncertainty of the source of the smoke disappeared when we approached the tower. It was engulfed in flames from the bottom to the top. The brave men were like fire ants all over the area. Some were pulling hoses while others were holding the hoses while in the broad stance spraying the tower from side to side putting the fire out. I was on my knees in the seat of the car moving around until they were no longer in view. Sliding back down on my backside saying, "Wow! They are so brave!"

The base was a city behind the gates. There was a commissary (what civilians would call a grocery store), a gas station (located not too far from the gate), and the ABC store was in sight. What we called, "The Exchange," was similar to a retail store with a florist inside. The beauty and barber shop were attached to the side very much like a strip mall. A hot dog stand that had steamed hot dogs and moist buns, had the best hot dogs ever. I liked mine plain while Sis had to have catsup, or she refused to eat it.

The cafeteria was across the street and not too far from it was a bowling alley. Mom and I ate at the cafeteria a few times but most of the time we did not take time to go and sit down and eat.

The movie theatre was close to one of the gates. I really liked being dropped there instead of going with Mom to her hair appointment. The National Anthem was always played at the beginning of the movie. It was automatically expected that everyone stood up (and they did). It was odd to go to the movies off the base because I expected to be standing, but the anthem was not played.

The lobby of the base theatre was shared with a large gym area. I would look through the open doors before the movie started. I heard the noise of basketballs being dribbled and the grunts of men when they went to take a shot, the squeaking of the tennis shoes running, then coming to a quick stop. Mostly though, I heard a lot of heavy breathing with the running and yelling out short words as if in some kind of male code known only to the players. Sometimes one or two of the sailors would come out running to the water fountain talking in the same code as they sipped then zipped back to this activity. They always had a serious look on their faces as though it may be a training for a life and death struggle with an enemy that I could not see. If they were there, they wore the same type of t-shirts, shorts, and squeaky tennis shoes all the others wore. It would have been difficult to identify the enemy in the building. The doors would swing open to the theatre and the sailors' games of whatever intrigue or ego left my mind all together.

There were many buildings that I did not know what went on inside of. Of course, there was a large area covered by docks loaded with chains, ropes, and different types of equipment. The docks were also painted—gray. The ships docked were several types such as destroyers, cruisers, submarines and the minesweepers that my dad was assigned to. The men serving on those wooden ships were called, "Iron Men." Their motto, *"Where the fleet goes, we've been."*

I always looked to see if any new ships had come in or if any ships had left. The destroyers were the largest of the ships at the Charleston base. They were easy to identify due to their impressive size.

Each level of the military had a club house with a bar and a dining room. Because Dad was a chief, our family took advantage of the CPO (Chief Petty Officers) Club. The dining room had tablecloths, white cloth napkins and candlelight. There was a dance floor and a place for a band or singer with a microphone in place a few steps down from the dining room. Families could have supper but if there were children it was required you were cleared out by 21:00 (9:00 p.m.). It is why I did not see anyone on the stage or set up at the tables surrounding the dance floor. Our family was long gone before that hour of fun and excitement ever began.

We were invited a few times to the Officers Club. It was set facing the Cooper River and was a white wooden building with many windows to show off the view. I knew it was time a dress, patent leather shoes, lace socks and most probably white gloves were to be adorned to attend the Officers Club. Our car would pull up to the front under the awning then two young men would open the doors to our car to help us out. One of the young men would slide into the driver's seat to go to park the car. I am sure as I am breathing that daddy most definitely did not want someone else to park his vehicle. There was no one that would take as great care and caution with his vehicles as he would, no doubt about it.

While not audible, the excitement was palpable. Mom, Selma, and I were escorted to the front door that was opened by another young man. They were dressed in long sleeve, white shirts with pleated fronts starched so heavily, I believe they could have stood to attention by themselves. They wore a black bow tie fastened at the neck, black pants with pressed creases in the front and black laced shoes so shiny they reflected whatever was near them. Another young man dressed in the same manner was inside waiting to seat us at a table. I do not recall why we were at the Officers Club or who we sat with because I was too enthralled with the atmosphere, soaking it all in. I watched the staff busily attending the fancy dressed people seated at the large round tables. I listened to the ice clink against the glasses as the water was poured and noticed how much brighter this dining area was in comparison to the CPO Club. It was due to the windows allowing sunlight to flood into the dining room at the Officers Club. The CPO Club had long heavy lined drapes that stayed pulled shut. It could be because the CPO Club looked out upon the recreation picnic shelter of the pool and the view at the Officers Club was of large oaks with Spanish moss draping off their limbs as if placed by an interior designer from Southern Living Magazine. The deep, thick green lawn peppered with brightly magenta-colored azaleas in bloom spread out to the banks of the Cooper River.

Mother reviewed with both of us girls, good manners before leaving the house. Daddy had reminded us to not speak at all, not even to each other unless an adult spoke to us first. It felt as though we were to be like dolls to be placed at the table but not to be played with, just there for decoration. It did not bother me at all if I could come in and sit in such a lovely place and watch the people. Honestly, I do not know if I ate anything. I do however know what it felt like to be walked to a table, have a chair held for me as I sat down and sat up straight with my best dress and a smile on my face. Dad complimented both of us when we were in the car at how well behaved, we were and how proud he was of us.

The officers did have a pool. There was quite a bit of thick green grass between the club and the pool. A high block wall with a top row of décor type block was on the club side. We had gone to the pool on a few occasions. The last time we went, Selma stood on the edge of the pool with the pool to her back. She jumped right in, hitting her chin on the way. She was bleeding. The lifeguard determined she needed to go to the hospital to have a couple of sutures placed—which leads me to add, also located on base there were medical offices, dental care office and an infirmary. A hospital was situated right outside one of the gates.

I had an opportunity to utilize both the infirmary and the emergency room all in one afternoon. I was at my favorite place on base—The Chief Petty Officers Pool. It was the best place to spend a day. Each summer we attended swimming lessons. The water was cold early in the morning, yet we would slip in the water no matter if our lips turned blue and our teeth chattered. I loved to swim, and the temperature was not going to be a deterrent. If thunder was heard in the background the wishing began to shoo it away so I would not have to exit the pool.

Some days mom would bring us back to the pool after lessons. There were days she would stay and stretch out in her bathing suit on her fold-out chair. She usually had three things with her, a book, her lipstick, and her sunglasses.

There were days she would drop us off as she did errands on base. It could be that she needed a break from hearing us yell, "Mama, watch me," each time we were on the diving board. It was one of those such days. I had seen her when she parked and tooted the horn to let me know she was coming to pick us up. I went over and grabbed my towel and started to walk toward the women's dressing room. I was eleven years old at the time. A boy (very blonde boy) from school walked up to me as I came up to the three-foot end of the pool. I could see my mom walking in. The boy reached over, placed his hand on my shoulder and shoved me into the pool. I lost my balance so with the towel I went in the water. There is not much room to go in the shallow end. My nose hit the bottom of the pool. Everything went dark as I was attempting to find my feet to stand up out of the water. I felt strong arms scoop me up and pull my entire body out of the water. I said, "I can't see. Mama, I can't see." It was true. Blood was coming out of my nose, and I am sure it frightened my mother because the source of the bleeding may not have been easily determined at that moment. Adding, her daughter was claiming a loss of vision. The next few minutes was a blur. Luckily, the infirmary was not far from the pool, so I was whisked over there to be evaluated. Evidently, with my mother in tow.

Later that evening I would come to know, hearing my mother recount the details to my dad, it was a Marine that jumped in rescuing me from floundering on the bottom of the pool. He carried me in his arms to the infirmary, only leaving when he felt I was going to be cared for.

The staff at the infirmary did a quick assessment and determined I needed to be assessed at the emergency room at the hospital. I was placed in the ambulance and a ride that would usually take ten to fifteen minutes was forty minutes due to the timing. It was a Friday, a payday and time for sailors, marines, and the shipyard to end their workday. Our transport decided for our own hearing to turn off the siren. No one could edge out of the way due to so many cars struggling to leave the gate.

Once we arrived and I was unloaded, the physician was there quickly to take care of whatever they were concerned about. I heard only whispers at the infirmary but could not make out the words. My vision had returned, yet I felt a pounding in my head. An ice bag had been placed on and off over my eyes.

Keep in mind, all I had on was a wet bathing suit. My towel was soaked, and I did not know where it went anyway. The air conditioning at a Charleston South Carolina Navy Base Hospital in July was working very well. It felt as though it was set to artic blast to me. My body was shaking so I attempted to roll up into a ball.

The doctor requested that I sit up in the exam chair. The chair was much like a dental chair that can be moved into different positions.

I straightened my arms beside me and stretched out my legs as far as I could, brought my head mid-line while my teeth began to chatter. The doctor asked someone in the room to go for a blanket. Oh, was that a relief to hear. He removed the pack from my face, placed his fingers on both sides of my upper nose and gave it a slight squeeze. The cold was no longer a concern as I felt an intense pain at the squeeze point. It was as my whole body of nerves had come to meet that one point. My stomach, not accustomed to experiencing such a sensation ever, ejected its contents-- spewing from my mouth as blood gushed from my nose and thick clots deposited out of my mouth. The doctor had stepped back missing the splatter caused by his touch to my nose, declaring, "Yep, it is broken." I did not ask, for I was sickened by what was all over my body and scared as I was bleeding from my nose and my mouth!

An orderly entered the room with, "It is too late for the blanket" blanket. He began to grab small white towels from a cabinet on the wall. Bringing them over to me first attempting to do what he could with my face, never mind what had settled in my long hair. Carefully placing towels over my throat, dropping one on my chest and tummy. He looked to my mother to help but she was asking the doctor, "What is broken?"

The doctor, stepping away further from the chair responded, "Her nose. It is her nose that is broken." Explaining he could take an x-ray but with the reaction just now, he was sure it was my nose. He went on to explain it broke evenly across indicated by no one sided knot. He gave instructions for care and then asked if there were any other questions before he let us go. I perked up as I was wiping up my chest that I had a question. Surprised, to hear me speak, the doctor turned his head toward me indicating his attention. I asked, "How about swimming? May I go swimming?" The doctor said that swimming was out for this summer. I began to cry and explain to him that we still had half the summer left and I loved to swim. I had never persisted for something on my own behalf before—and I did so out of need—not thinking beforehand of what to say, just pleading to not take away swimming for the summer.

The doctor stood quietly contemplating. He spoke, "I tell you what. You can go swimming on one condition." I barely took a breath awaiting his words. "You have to wait two weeks before you swim—*and no diving*, not from the board, or the side of the pool. No jumping in. Your nose can not handle the pressure caused by diving. Can you promise that?" I said, "Yes, as long as I can still swim." I believe the poor orderly was relieved for my mother to take me out the door to home.

The next day I looked at the calendar and clarified with Mom on the date I could return to the pool. My sister piping in that did not mean she had to wait two weeks to go to the pool. She was reassured that did not apply to her and yes, she could go swimming. Although mom offered for me to go along when she took my sister during those two weeks, I opted to stay home. I felt it would be torturous to just sit in the picnic area and watch others swim.

You see, swimming was more than just splashing around in the water on a hot day. I was enamored with taking a dive off the board. I would paddle as far to the twelve-foot bottom as I could go. The goal was to be able to touch the bottom. I tried to swim further out so I did not keep the next person on the board from having their turn. It took several attempts of diving deeper, kicking quickly and using my hands and arms to propel me to touch the bottom.

What was found at the bottom was a different place of space. It was darker. I noticed the quiet all around me. There were no other bodies, no laughing from other children or whistles from the lifeguard—just quiet. I delayed my return to the surface as long as possible, sort of just floated slowly back up. I took my fingers and ran them through my long blonde hair to make it float out all around my head. As the surface became closer, the muffled sounds slipped through as did the filtered sunshine. Once I broke through the water barrier, all was as it was before I dove in just moments before. How can it be? I experienced something in the depths that I liked. It was soothing yet exciting as if I was the only one that knew of how to transcend from a current and trivial activity to another place all together. I now liken it to a spiritual moment.

Although, the diving had to end for that summer, I would pick up the next summer taking dives like this throughout my childhood. I never shared the feeling or how much I liked the experience with anyone. I have thought of that type of quiet and the sight of the sun shining above beckoning a return. Perhaps it is like the bright light some talk about when so close to death. For me, the light was welcoming but I knew all the noise and commotion would come with it.

I am aware I am not a mermaid. I do not possess gills, so residing in the tranquility of the sea, somewhere between the depths at the point the sun's rays still penetrate, and the chaos and sounds the world offers on the surface, is not an option.

My mother loved to use some sort of quote or analogy to guide you along. She offered," Wanda Lynn, there are times that you swim too deep in the water," Adding, "Sometimes it is good to come up and just swim on the surface and do surface stuff." Great advice from someone that dwelt in the deep, frozen waters of the artic.

***

Selma and Wanda on Race Day
Outside Military Unit

The Military Housing Community

There was housing on base and housing units together in a community off base. The 1960's to 1970's, off base navy housing did not have a gate or guard checking to see that only military personnel entered the complex. People from nearby neighborhoods could access the grounds as could anyone else. This soon became problematic. The residents started complaining of items stolen. It was highly doubtful that another military person committed the thefts because the punishment would have been severe.

There were benefits to living in navy housing and one of them had been the safety of the military families and their possessions. Our family was not afforded that safety. It took both our car (a pale yellow 1966 GTO black hard top with black pinstripes down the side) and the shiny chrome wheels along with the tires from his prized 1966 Ford truck (same pale yellow and delicately pinstriped by his own hand)—to be stolen— for dad to opt out from housing.

The car being swiped from its parking place right outside our front door could have been stopped. I saw the three teenagers push our car down the road when it was still daylight. Kids were outside playing, not have being called in for supper yet. I went in and told my mother that boys were pushing our car down the road toward the playground but she just said, "Umm hmm" as the spatula flipped over whatever was frying in the large cast iron pan. I guess avoiding being splattered by grease was more distraction than a yelling kid telling you this and that every few minutes. It took a sheriff's deputy pounding on the door to shake us all out of bed to grab the attention of dad and mom that indeed the car had been stolen.

The deputy explained, the boys had taken it on a "joy ride" and evidently were caught when they wrecked the car. Never hearing those words before, it certainly did not sound like a lot of fun to me (and certainly not for our car). There was also the matter of five dollars of my birthday money I had left in the car that was spent by those mean boys! I had saved it even when I wanted to spend it on the model of the Apollo 11 at the Pinehaven Shopping Center earlier that day.

My dad went to view the damages the next day. He was not much for giving the details except to say there was candy stuck all over the inside. The windows had been left rolled down overnight and it rained, soaking the car. I believe he was quite choked up to look at the car he had taken such tender care of, sitting in an impound yard all soaking wet and ruined. Heck, he had even washed the engine. No other dad ever lifted the hood and spit shined the engine of their car. At least not that I have ever seen.

The next incident is clear in my mind as if it happened this morning. It was a warm morning but not yet hot enough to hear the sizzle sound when the heat was rising up off the road. I was getting my bike out of the back yard to ride to school when the Chief went out to head off to work. He held the tall wooden gate open. The latch was at the top, much higher than I could reach. Although I usually tried to avoid my dad because he made me feel all jittery, not because he was going to hit me, but I just felt like I was like a bee buzzing and he wanted to swat me out of the way.

This day was like any other, felt like I was buzzing and slowing him down, but it was nice to have someone tall enough to open the latch. As the gate opened, you could see past the grayish asphalt back road used for parking. The marsh stretched out just beyond the road (the sand having little circular holes where fiddler crabs popped in and out of all day). The marsh grasses, ever changing with the season, were now black on the bottom and greening up on the top spiking up toward a hazy bluish sky with the blending in of the calm Ashley River.

Dad with starched, pressed, and creased khaki uniform with ribbons all pinned to his chest, suddenly froze in place, like we were playing freeze tag. No way had he just been touched and decided to stop in place like a frozen statue until another runner came by to tag and unfreeze him. You see, the Chief did not play those games even if we begged, so he surely was not playing on his way to work.

Nope, this time daddy was not sorrowful at what he was viewing. He was as mad as I had ever seen him. Remember the cartoon bull on Looney Tunes—the one that turned red blowing smoke out of flaring nostrils with a ring pierced in the center—his head lowered as he stomped hooves into the ground right before he became a locomotive to run over the object of what was stirring his heated anger? Yep, that cartoon bull was pale pink compared to the color of red my dad had turned as he methodically moved around his truck taking stock of his pride and joy pickup sitting up on cinder blocks.

Not only were the tires gone, so were the chrome wheels so shiny they could serve as a mirror. No fingerprints, no smudges nor black marks and certainly no dust could be detected on the Chief's set of wheels due to the hours he spent squatting beside them and wiping them down with some secret concoction from a flattened round can aided by an old t-shirt.

I pedaled happily off as the Chief dealt with the dilemma of the snatched wheels. If those crooks were ever captured, I did not hear anything about it. I can say if the Chief would have caught them, the marsh may have had other decaying matter to sink and repurpose.

Knowing that folks had stolen one vehicle and violated another, the decision was "We are out of here!" This time the Mayflower team did not transfer us for it was just a few miles down the road.

***

Hanging Out in the Woods — 1972

The Ache for a Home is in All of Us
The safe place we can go as we are and not be questioned
—Maya Angelou

This new neighborhood, Wando Woods was just down the road from housing—a place where we came to know as home base. It had not only military families. There were civilian families residing in houses too, no apartment houses to be seen. These were stand-alone houses with dogs in large yards, some were two-stories, and one lucky kid had a trampoline in her yard.

Dad drove us into the driveway of a three-bedroom white brick house. A garage attached to the house and a larger matching brick garage stood next to a large oak tree in the chain linked and gated back yard. A clothesline stretched out three lines almost the length of the yard. A cement pad had been poured underneath with placement on the sunny side of the yard. This was a great improvement to the hexagon twirling clothesline mom dried our clothes on in navy housing.

I pleaded with my dad and my mom to "please, pretty please" have my own room so not to share with my messy sister. After all, we were older now and this house did have three bedrooms. It did not take long to know that the dream was lost. The roll away bed, stand up stereo and mountains of books all read by my mother were placed in the extra bedroom.

No amount of wishing would keep it from being assigned as a guest bedroom, although we rarely had anyone stay over anyway. The only person ever to stay was my grandfather—my dad's dad. He was a truck driver of one of those big semi-trucks and trailers. He must have driven all over. Maybe once a year, if he was delivering something near where we were living, he would drop by and stay the night, leaving in the morning before anyone woke up. My sister and I would find a dollar stuck under the corner of our placement when we sat down for breakfast. Quick visit, almost like he was not ever there. Hard to get to know someone that pops in and out of your life like Santa Claus.

The closet in the guestroom came to house dad's extra uniforms, a few blankets, and some boxes. The small green suitcase—the type used for overnight stays—I can hear the latches click, first one then the other (rarely both at the same time). It was lodged on the top left side of the shelf, and it belonged to my mother. I knew she cherished the contents. It was heavy and full of papers with my mother's handwriting. Mother had taken a creative writing class at the College of Charleston. It makes plenty of sense, given that she loved to read, that she may like to write stories. I did not understand at the time she had plenty to write about just living her life.

There were as many kids (if not more) to meet and make friends with, in this neighborhood, as in navy housing. There were two boys that lived next door. The oldest brother found out my name and wrote on his white t-shirt, *David loves Wanda*. No pressure either as this happened on the day we moved in.

Our large garage in the back yard became a check-in place during the summer. It did not have cars or equipment in it. It stayed closed most of the time. Selma or I would raise the door some and the side door was unlocked when we were out there. The temperature was cooler than the yard because it was dark before we raised the door.

There was a yellow plastic radio with a grid over the speaker, a dial to turn to locate your favorite radio station. Most of the kids liked WTMA, an AM station playing the new hits out of Charleston. It was playing during the day as kids came by to hang out and chat. It was especially exciting when one of the cute boys in the neighborhood would enter the back gate. It was in that garage that I learned how to talk to boys and stopped being so scared of them.

Now, do not go and get the idea that the garage was some sort of make out shack because it certainly was not. My dad would have blown a gasket if he even caught a whiff of such a thing happening. Besides, my mother was at home. She would come out what seemed like every few minutes to update all of us uninterested kids on the Watergate trial. She was so impressed with Senator Sam Irvin from North Carolina and the Speaker of the House, Tip O'Neill. Looking back, she was probably attempting to enlighten us about democracy and the fact was she had no one else to talk to about it.

***

The Road in the Woods

1973

On July 5th 1973, I happened to have come inside the house as the phone rang and of course I pounced on it. It was David Eadie. He was calling from Ronnie's house, a few blocks away. He told me he was coming over and would be there in a few minutes. Then he called me a nanny goat before he hung up the phone. David and I had liked each other for a while. He recently rode a pony over to our house which drew Selma's attention. She was offered a ride and then she and David were liking one another. This was not the first time of my sister scooping up a boy I liked before I stopped liking them.

David had a cowlick that made his sandy blonde hair stick up at his hairline on one side. He was so excited that he was soon going to have braces to help with an overbite. He was outgoing and comfortable talking to everyone, including girls. He wrote me letters when I was in North Carolina visiting my Aunt Inez earlier that summer.

I was a skittish type of girl. If a boy came on too strong, I would back away quickly. Most often I ended the relationship without giving too much of a reason. If my sister and recent boyfriend liked each other it did not bother me—much.

This summer day was sizzling hot. You know when you look at the road and see a haze rising. A sizzle is heard like when cold butter hits a hot frying pan coming from the sun baking the black asphalt. It is more likely than not to have summer days with that type of unrelenting heat in the low country.

Selma and I were waiting on David and whoever was riding bikes with him to be there in minutes, but minutes went, and no one was riding down the road. At first, we thought they were hanging over at Ronnie's longer than expected because his dad had a race car shop, and everyone likes to see a real race car.

Suddenly an odd thing occurred, the sound of screeching sirens coming down the main street of our neighborhood (Paramount Road). Ronnie road up on his bike and said he did not know why David or his friend were not riding with him. He reported they had left his house right after David called our house.

Some of the boys had biked to where the sirens were headed to, but the police stopped them. It was one block down from where we lived. The boys kept trying to maneuver around to get to see something or hear something. Paramount and other streets nearby had been blocked off. One of the brothers living next door had ridden down to the incident site. He had talked to one of the neighbors who lived close by and came back with an unexpected report. A car had been speeding down Paramount and David was crossing the road on his bike. His friend went ahead and crossed the street. David decided to turn back to avoid the car. The car hit him—no word if he was ok.

Many of the kids on bikes and others walked over to our house where we waited for word on David. My mother was right there with us encouraging good thoughts. I had thought he may have broken his arm or possibly his leg. Mom helped me call the hospital he was taken to for care. The nurse asked if I was family and I had to tell her the truth, "No ma'am, I am one of his friends." She told me they were not allowed to give out information except to members of patient's families. I felt deflated as I hung up. Somehow, it did not seem real until I spoke to a nurse. Heck, it was today when I spoke with him on the phone. I told the friends waiting what the nurse had told me. So, we waited.

The neighborhood boys continued to ride close to the scene but not to the point where the police had to warn them to get away. My mother answered any questions any of us came up with and perhaps she was being positive so that we all would have hope that our friend was going to be alright.

After many hours, one of the bike riders said, all the police, roadblocks, and the ambulance were gone. I asked Mom if I could go down there, and she granted permission. Strangely, despite how supportive she had been, she did not accompany me. It was later in the afternoon and maybe she needed to get supper started.

My neighbor rode his bike as I walked. He rode slowly and pedaled circles around me until we arrived a block down. He dismounted and walked his bike as we surveyed the road and the area around it. We were trying to make sense of all of this. Thinking out loud, my neighbor pointed out the route they were riding. There was a road where they would have been coming from, attempting to cross catty-cornered up a slight hill to the next street. It would have been a tough choice to go across or turn back if a car was coming.

What I saw at the scene left little to the imagination that the outcome was not going to be a broken arm or leg. David, like many boys had a ten-speed bicycle. The speedometer was on the far side of the road in the grass—just lying there, as was one of his high-top converse tennis shoes.

Noticing his *one* shoe left there in the grass gave me a sinking feeling. Why would his shoe be there instead of on his foot? It would not have been left behind if he needed to wear it. His other shoe was nowhere to be seen. It certainly was not setting beside his lone shoe like a pair would be when taken off together.

By this late in the afternoon the haze and sound of the sizzle were gone. The shade from the trees covered and cooled the area. I slipped off my shoe to feel the heat of the pavement, wondering how long he had to lie there on that scorching black top. How long was our friend in the road before someone helped him up?

The skid marks were short, ending just beyond the place the shoe had come to rest. I was not panicked. I was not crying, not a tear puddled up in my eyes. The feeling is best described as no feeling, as if you are there looking at these left behind items, but you are not really there at all.

I looked up to see if cars where coming as I walked out into the street. The only sound I could hear was a ringing in my ears. It sounded much like the sizzle earlier that day but steady, not fading and rising in volume. I wanted to see just beyond where the skid marks stopped. My friend pointed down toward the road not far from where I was standing. There in the pavement was a tooth, slightly pressed down in the pavement. Another tooth mark beside it yet without a tooth in its in-dention. All I could think of at that moment was how happy David was about get-ting braces. The "no feeling" was accompanied by dizziness and a need to vomit.

Walking at a slow and steady pace with my neighbor walking his bike silently beside me, I arrived home and went straight to my room and laid down on my bed. Mother came in and started to ask questions but went for a cool washcloth placing on my forehead. Somehow, avoiding vomiting, I fell asleep.

When I woke up, mom came in my room. She told me she had received a call from someone in David's family. They had the number from when I called the hospital. She went on to say, she was told David died. As a twelve-year-old boy, what do you do with that kind of information? I did not know what to do with it, or what to say, or how to feel about it at all.

We were told it was only David that had been hit. His friend who came with him made it across the street safely, but he saw the whole accident. You know we never saw or heard from that boy again. He was not in school when we started back. I heard his family had moved away.

The boy was not at the funeral home or the funeral. I looked for him and did not see him. My parents had a discussion if my sister and I should go to either of the gatherings. My mom had received a call, again from someone in David's family asking if it was OK with her if a photo of me and one of my sister, was placed in David's pocket to be buried with him. It was the request that prompted mother to discuss not only the request but also if Selma or I wanted to attend either service.

Again, not knowing what to expect given my age and not ever attending a service or going to a funeral home to pay respects meant I was scared. My photo being placed in his pocket did not bother me. I wondered if I was going to have that sickening feeling or the "no feeling" with ringing in my ears.

A couple of days passed, then came the time to go to the funeral home. It was in the evening and church clothes were required of course. My mother took me and honestly, I do not recall my sister attending. She was given the option to at-tend or not. Perhaps she decided not to be there. She too had agreed her picture could be placed in David's pocket but as I mentioned I believe she opted out of the services.

MY MOTHER'S SUITCASE

When my mother pulled into the parking lot of the funeral home it was already quite full of cars. We sat in the car for a few minutes as mom explained that there would be a casket although she expected it would be closed (adding it was up to me if I wanted to go up to the casket). She gave me the permission to make that decision on my own, telling me it was no right or wrong way. Mom told me we could leave anytime to just let her know. The review over, we opened the car doors and headed towards the door where everyone else was entering.

Inside, there were separate rooms for families that had loved ones recently deceased. The lighting was dim and the smell of carnations filled the hallway, becoming stronger when you entered the family room. There were men in black suits, starched collars with a faint smile on their faces, opening doors and directing visitors to the correct family room. A stand with an attached overhead light shining down on an open book to sign in stood outside the family room's door. Mom signed in once we reached the entrance. There was a line to this family's room. Once we entered the room, I could see a casket at the other end. The casket top was open. I reached out for my mother's hand and pulled down on it so she would lean over. In an urgent, lowered voice through gritted teeth I stared over and said, "The casket is open!" She reminded me, I could choose not to go to the casket, and I could leave at any time. Settling myself, I thought I needed to be more adult about this and continue. I would make up my mind once I reached where David was lying.

Before the casket were a few people hugging those in the line. I noticed one of them was David's brother. A woman sat in a chair with others standing on either side of her. Her eyes were swollen. Reasoning she was David's mother. My mom went before I did in line. She bent at the waist to introduce herself and tell her who I was. The woman's face changed as she looked at me to a saddened joy. She stretched out both arms. I could not refuse to allow this grieving mother to hug me. I took a couple of steps then she wrapped her thin arms around me. She slightly rocked me while patting my back as she wept. She pulled herself away yet kept a hold of my upper arms as she looked at me and said, "Thank you. You know David liked you a whole lot. I am so glad you came by." I nodded as she dropped her hold and blew her nose into a cloth handkerchief wadded up in her right hand. My protective "No feeling," turned into a sorrowful feeling for his poor mama.

The next few steps led to the decision about the casket. Mom squeezed my hand and bent to look me in the eye. "It is your choice. No one is going to be mad or sad if you choose not to go up there," she reminded me. I looked at her deep brown eyes and asked if she would go with me and to please hold my hand. She gently nodded.

We slowly approached the place where David was lying in this long, maple colored, wooden box, a light directed to the top part of the casket. There was white, silky ruffled material lining the casket and a small pillow made of the same material. I looked at the body as a whole, first. I could not believe it, there he was, this active, talkative boy in a suit. I do not know what I expected, but a suit sure was not it, (a blue suit with red plaid lapels). He did not have on his t-shirt and jeans. I mean it is all I had ever seen him in. I bet someone had to go and buy this suit because I am pretty darn sure he would have refused to wear it if he were alive. That is the point, he is not alive, and his mama felt like he needed to be placed in a suit.

I then readied myself to look at the details. While being shocked at his suit, I had noticed his left thumb was missing. The guise to hide its missing by tucking it under his right hand was a good move but a miss, nonetheless. I guess the funeral home did the best they could with his condition. Besides having what appeared to be a ton of makeup on his face to even out the damage, his head was misshapen, sunken in some places. Then I noticed, Lord help me, as I squeezed my mother's hand, his cowlick, once so prominent was no longer there!

I squeezed a little bit harder on my mom's hand, as I looked away from what was supposed to be my friend's face. Mom looked at my face and guided me to take steps away from the box with my friend's shell. He was no longer here with us or in that box.

Mom did not ask if I was ready to leave, I guess moms can look at you and see those things. My chest ached with a deep heaviness. My ears had that sizzling sound, and my stomach had a few complaints of its own. I felt light on my feet as my mother guided me in another direction. She pushed on a door that led us into the ladies' restroom. She grabbed some paper towels on our way to the sink while still holding unto my hand. Turning on the cold water, she wet and squeezed out the paper towel and began pressing it to my face and forehead. Inga took another paper towel, wet it, and placed it on the back of my neck. Slowly, the ringing subsided, and my stomach decided not to lurch out of my mouth. The deep ache where my heart is located had not vacated but at least the uneasiness in my mother's face did go away.

She hummed one of her Norwegian tunes for a little while. Women were coming in and out the rest room. Mother nodded at them. When I looked up in the mirror and met my mother's eyes she mouthed, "You are okay now, yes?" I managed a slight smile and a nod. Ever so easily pivoted to face my mom, opening my arms, I wrapped them around her and hugged her saying softly, "Thank you." She kissed the top of my head, grabbed my hand again, just in case, as we found the closest exit. The summer night air is rarely a relief for it hangs with a soggy thickness clinging to your skin, but on that night, it was welcomed. It was an escape from the smell of carnations and almost acting as a cure for heavy hearts and sick stomachs. My earlier ailments resolved, yet now were replaced by a banging headache. Mother turned off the radio. It was a good thing home was not far away.

The next day my friend was laid to rest at the cemetery next to the navy housing where our family had lived. It was a beautiful spot under the shade of a big, strong oak. One of those that have limbs reaching out so far it looks like it wants to give you a hug. At least that is the way I look at them. There was a view of the Ashley River from his spot. And it was far enough away from when the golfers come to plunk balls into the river that his spot would not get stepped on.

I attended the services, but I chose not to go up to the casket. I knew my friend was no longer there. His mama was crying so much she had to be helped by two people to get up from where she was sitting to go out to the car that was carrying her and the family to the graveyard.

I did think of him as I stood there not being able to hear enough of what the pastor was saying to make sense. I stopped listening and started recalling our last talk when he called me a nanny goat and laughed. I thought of the last time I saw him when he brought over his pony. It was when he told me he was going to have braces put on and how happy he was. Yes, I tuned out all that sadness and realized I had always seen him smiling his big toothy, confident grin. I thought that is what I want to remember of my friend.

*＊＊

Leftovers and Starving in Norway

Inga did not talk about her being a little girl or what it was like living in a country at war. She was not heard saying how easy Selma and I had it compared to her childhood. We did not know she was a hungry little girl eating tree bark or making blood pancakes from the drippings of the farm animals. There was not a comment when she was encouraging Selma and I to clean our plates at dinner about *her* starving.

She would mention that we were fortunate to have food and to consider the starving children in China who would be happy to have the food. We heard that so often, I thought then let's send the hungry children in China the food, I am full.

I was what my mom called a puny child (slender and very picky about food). It would be identified today as OCD, obsessive compulsive disorder, because I did not like any of my food to touch, even though I knew it was all going to meet up in the same place. I also ate all of one serving of food before moving on to the next. For example, I would eat every kernel of corn before eating my mashed potatoes. I did not have the specific pattern every time I ate. The first pick would be whatever food was closet to me on the plate or the color that was most pleasant.

The rules were not to put on your plate any more than you could eat. I did a good job of measuring it out for myself, however, someone heaving a big heaping spoonful of something you did not choose for yourself for the very reason that you would not eat it, is annoying. The battle ensues between parent and child. The child (me): "I do not like it. I am not going to eat it. I did not place it on my plate." The parent (my mother): "It is good for you. You need to try new foods. You are too puny. It will help build your system up. Eat it. OK? Try at least one bite." It never goes well when an hour later you are still sitting there with a plate with cold food in front of you. The green brussel sprouts messed up by touching the peas and colliding in the rice—a whole meal—and your small appetite ruined. So, you were told one of two things. Either; the plate will be wrapped up and saved for your next meal, (oh yay!) or, excuse yourself, no one is at the table by this time anyway, go wash up and go to bed. Parent, (always mom) "No TV. You did not eat your supper. You know there are children starving in China."

There was never one word about the gnawing she felt as a child. Not a tear fell remembering when the soldiers would have a skin and bone, tiny slip of a girl, jump up like a dog begging for scraps of her family's own food supply—holding it out of her reach—higher and higher with each jump while laughing and saying teasing words in German, "Bitte, bitte."

Decades later she revealed she always felt guilty for acting like a circus dog. Selma Andrea, her mother had told her to stay away from the SS. It would have disappointed her knowing she had performed for those men for bits of bread. No explaining of eating blood pancakes. Flour scrounged up while preparing the soldiers food. The drippings of the slaughtered farm animals were used instead of milk (which was so difficult to obtain). The soldiers did not care about what they left behind after they engulfed everything in sight to fill their bellies and keep themselves healthy and strong.

If I had known her story, would I have eaten a green, slimy ball that smelled bad dumped on my plate, mixed in with other foods? Probably not. Maybe if I had known some of the story, I may have chosen to try other items and maybe she would not have heaved them on my plate. I certainly would have looked at her and food differently.

Each time she received a package from Norway she would call out our names and ask Selma and me if we would like some sardines or goat cheese. We would say, "No", and run to our room. Once, chocolate was added to the list she called out and before she could lift her head to listen for an answer, we were standing to her side waiting for a piece of luscious, milky chocolate. Each taking a piece, we wandered off to the living room to experience a sweet treat, unwrapping first the blue with gold laced color paper wrapping, and then delicately easing the gold foil back to reveal the chocolate. Selma looked at me, both wondering if the chocolate, being a darker color than any chocolate we had seen before, was a good or a not-so-good thing. How bad could it be, it is chocolate?

We agreed to take a bite on the count of three. One, two, three—both chomped down on the Norwegian delight. Again, we looked at one another. This time with our tongues sticking out and our noses wrinkled getting up to run to the bathroom. I was closer, so made it to the sink first. Spitting it out as I was turning on the sink faucet to rinse my mouth out. Grabbing my toothbrush to scrub out any of the bitterness out and away from me. Selma went into the half bath in Mom and Dad's room doing the same as I was but with a bit more drama. The choking sounds and the word yuck being said loudly. Sis and I adding, "This is disgusting," lured mother from the kitchen table to investigate what all the fussing was about. Mother noted, Selma was acting as if she had been poisoned. She kept it up by replying, "I have been poisoned by that nasty chocolate." Mother, not offended, kind of laughed and dismissed our dislike of her homeland's chocolate as a lack of our taste buds for the finer things in life. "You Americans"—she used that term when she was going to make a comparison as if we were her enemy—"You Americans, do not know what good chocolate is because all you have is milky chocolate with a lot of sugar. Norwegian chocolate is pure and good and does not make you fat." Before I could catch the words, they slid right out, "You do not get fat eating this chocolate because no one eats it. It tastes so bad." She smiled and nodded heading back to rummage in her gifts from home. It was not long before my sister and I heard our names called out asking if we wanted some sardines—goat cheese —laughing to the point she could barely say it—chocolate? We sounded together instantly, "No," running to our room. Mom laughed uncontrollably from the kitchen table.

***

A dinner and a show may not be such a treat. Our kitchen table was the setting for considerable drama varying on type and degree of severity. My mother had taught my sister and I how to set the table with placement of the plates to the glasses. The silverware to be set on a certain side of the plate in a particular order, turned in a specific direction. The table always had a pressed tablecloth. The silver candlesticks held lit candles at every dinner time regardless the fare, ranging from hotdogs to roast beef stewed with potatoes and carrots flavored with a bay leaf or two. Not many southern dishes were served at our table.

My dad would be at home most of the time for dinner, only to hurry out the door to the race car shop immediately after he had eaten. If there were any topics he needed to address, it would be done between bites.

Our report cards were reviewed during this time. Selma had been a straight "A" student since the beginning. Dad would take this time to praise her as if it was a coronation. She did not bring a book home, never studied for a test, yet her grades were perfect.

I did well but did not come into the "all As" set until fifth grade. It was a concerted effort to prove I could do as well as my younger sister. It required sacrificing many after school hours to study. It was nice to hear the praise although I still was not crowned, "Queen of Elementary Academia."

Dad would take this time to correct our table manners. Even though Selma was his obvious golden daughter, he banged his fists on the table when she placed her elbows on the table. My startle reflex sent a ripple through my nervous system as the whole table moved after hearing the clink of silverware as it jumped from the force of the pounding. Selma quickly removed her elbows as the vibrations ripped through like an earthquake.

There was a time he got up from his place at the table, walked over to where Selma was seated at the other end of the table, knocked her elbows off the table and her off balance. It set the tone for such a lovely dinner.

Once, he chose to discuss notes found in my pants pockets that had to have been given to him by my mother (after all, she did the laundry). The simple notes passed in class among students to reach a certain boy to a certain girl. "I like you. If you like me or not check the box." A box would be drawn beside the words YES or NO. Of course, what he thought was teasing, I found humiliating.

I put my fork in its proper place, laid my hands in my lap while dropping my head. The goal was not to cry at the table. A lump formed in my throat made it not only hard to swallow but hard to breathe. The tears would alternate streaming down each cheek. Dad's response was to take his leave claiming I could not take a little teasing.

Do not misunderstand, Dad was not the only one taking stage at the kitchen table. My mother had been fuming about something but waited until the spaghetti was prepared and served up to pick up her plate and throw it against the wall behind her. It shattered and pieces of chinaware splintered in all directions, noodles stuck to the wall and sauce fell into a clump onto the desk below.

As you may have guessed, I did not enjoy dinner time unless it was at a restaurant. People are not as apt to cause a scene in public as they seem so comfortable to do at home where they are accustomed to hitting all their marks on the stage they know so well.

* * *

A Catalog to Wish Upon

The Sears and Roebuck Company put into circulation a catalog called a "Wish Book" during the Christmas seasons annually. It was full of all types of toys and treasures for a child's heart to desire. Composed of large glossy pages, it was heavy, yet no one complained once their turn came to look at all it had to offer. I am not sure how parents viewed this wonderful edition for the holiday season. It could be seen as helpful as a child decided what he or she may want Santa to bring depending on the report of their behavior throughout the year. Perhaps, many parents saw future disappointment for the long lists their good little son or daughter would be inspired to write after seeing all the toys offered up that would be too costly to be provided in Santa's big red bag.

My list had one item consistently listed for three years—roller skates. I had doubled my chances as if it were a lottery being played by asking for the skates on my birthday as well. I wanted to not wear the rented skates at the skate rink. They smelled. Their color was tan with numbers clearly visible on the heels easily seen as you skate along. The rented skates often rubbed a section of your foot causing a blister due to so much wear and tear by so many skaters. The footbeds did not conform to my own foot not allowing for precision turning. Then, sometimes the wheels would be sticky or would become stuck and not turn, causing a risk of falling. No matter whether I pleaded these points or how well I had attempted to behave, the gift of skates eluded me for three years.

Finally, an elf must have proofread my letter and noted the repeats for nothing else but a pair of skates, listing the cost and page number in the "Wish Book." The skates appeared at Christmas. The feeling of "Yay for me, at last!" I was more than anxious until I could go to the rink with my very own skates. I could not use them outside for the wheels would not be allowed at the rink. I placed them on my feet and stood up in them every day until the Friday arrived. I tied the laces together placed them over my shoulder and walked to where the bus would stop to take the kids from nearby streets to Goose Creek. A church owned the skating rink and sent a bus to transportation to the rink. I felt so free as I took the floor in *my own skates.* They did not stink, and they moved where I pushed them to go. The "Wish Book," always held a place in my heart for putting a picture to my wish.

Santa brought us three speed bikes when we had asked for ten speeds. Oh, how we tried not to show disappointment on our faces that year. I do not think we were too successful given that my mother took us outside to point out all the good things about the matching deep hunter green girl bikes. They stayed in excellent shape with no scratches, dents, or rust. We did not ride the bikes. They stayed in the big garage away from the elements. I realize it seems both Selma and I were ungrateful brats not realizing how hard our parents worked and saved to purchase items for us. Not to excuse our not liking the bikes, I just as soon ride my old blue bike or borrow my neighbor's ten speed. A grand example is if Ralphie from "A Christmas Story" had received a water gun instead of the coveted Red Rider BB Gun. As a friend once explained to me about a bad choice she had made, "The heart wants what the heart wants."

* * *

Selma also had a long waiting wish. She too had written Santa about an item she was dreaming about. She had added to her birthday wishes and became persistent in asking for it every few weeks. It too was listed in the "Wish Book." Honestly, I truly never believed her wish would appear anywhere near our Christmas tree or our house. Boys had asked for similar toys and had been disappointed, so her chances were slim to none despite the women's movement.

Even if by some slight, rare chance she should receive it, where would she use it? If you have not guessed by now, her wish was motorized. Selma had been persistent with her request. I thought it was pushy but hey she was proof that, "the squeaky wheel gets the oil." She was wishing, begging, pleading for a go-cart.

Mom and Selma went to visit Dad's family in North Carolina during July fourth week. Dad came home with a go-cart for Selma planning to gift it to her when she came home although it was a few weeks before her birthday. The owner of the race car and his boys had bought a go-cart as well. The next day Dad, his friend, his boys, and I went to an empty parking lot to try out the new carts.

Everyone had driven the two carts then Dad turned to me and asked if I would like to drive it. I had been standing, watching everyone, and wishing there was a bathroom nearby. Not a good thing when you are the only female in the group. Of course, I wanted to drive the go-cart! I hopped in with few instructions, never had driven anything motorized, closest thing was a push mower. I made a few rounds. I knew they were timing me because they had been timing one another. Dad signaled for me to take another lap. Our course was set by going around four light poles with three-foot cement bases. I had gotten to the third pole and as Dad reported to me, I lost traction due to the speed I was going. The cart lifted off its wheels and slammed into the base of the pole.

I do not remember the wreck, thank goodness. The next thing I knew is I woke up in our bathtub at home with Dad talking to me. He helped me dry off and go to bed. It was a night for fireworks, so I was awakened with my head pounding. It was dark outside. Dad came in and prepared me some soup, crackers, and a coke in a glass. My head was hurting to the point I felt nauseous, so I skipped the soup and crackers. I took my left hand, wrapped it around the glass to take a sip of cola. As I lifted the glass, I lost my grasp, the glass hit the table and the coke spilled everywhere. I started to cry while standing the glass up and saying, "I am so sorry, Daddy." He quietly reassured me and dried off my hands, directing me back to bed. He told me not to worry, he would clean it up.

Later, not able to rest because of the whistles and booming of the fireworks, I looked out the kitchen window to see my dad out hammering on the frame of the go-cart. My sister was due home the next day and I am sure he wanted to repair it.

Eventually, I fell asleep. The next morning, I met Dad in the kitchen and asked him if the cart was fixed. He said, "Yes, I stayed up all night, but I have it ready." First Selma came home, and Dad presented her with the wished-for gift. Sis came in and told me, "Thanks for wrecking my go-cart before I even got to drive it." I just stood there still in my nightgown in the middle of the day. Mother had come in as soon as she arrived to check on me. My head was hurting still, as was my left forearm whenever I moved it a certain position. The truth is, there was a navy hospital located nearby and there would not have been any charges due to Dad's military active-duty service. It would have been very reasonable to take your unconscious daughter to be evaluated. I did not understand why Dad did not take me to the hospital. Was he concerned what Mom would say if he had me admitted? Would the wreck cause the go-cart to be shelved and Dad would lose his money? Perhaps, it would change the plans he had with his friends. I just did not know and did not ask.

The next day Dad, his friends and sons went out with Selma this time to drive the cart. She made a point to inform me she did not wreck it like I had.

There were other opportunities to drive the cart at a closed cart track and also at the Summerville Speedway. On a day when there were not any races scheduled; Rachel, her brother, Selma, Tommy and Glen were the young set to drive the track. Dad and his friends also took turns. I had attended and Dad encouraged me to get behind the wheel. I still had the post wreck pain in my head. I drove out on the track, but the slope frightened me. I steered to the bottom more level part, bringing the cart in after the third turn. I came in through the level pit road, stopping close to where my dad was standing. When I took the helmet off, I heard him say to his friend, "It was too bad she wrecked. I think she would have been the best little driver of all of them." I know it was not meant for me to hear. The statement gave me a bit of a boost and disappointment. I continued to go skating but the cart racing thrill was gone.

My sister's cart was in the back garage with strict instructions to not take it out without dad. Selma saw some of the boys ride their mini-bikes and she was not to be outdone despite the instructions. She would push the cart out of the garage to the end of the road so mom would not hear her start it up. She would get it started and drive around the neighborhood. It made me nervous because I was concerned that she would get caught. She would cut it off at the end of the road and push it back in the garage. No adult ever contacted our parents to tell on her excursions. She laughed at me when I told her not to take the chance.

Selma and I had started drifting apart. It was not because I had wrecked her go-cart. We had a different group of friends, participated in different activities. There was also that fact that she betrayed secrets a sister should not tell. When I started my monthly cycle, she immediately went outside to report the grand news, very loudly to the brothers next door. Heaven only knows why she did such a thing. Maybe she thought it was funny or she just wanted the attention to tell such personal things. I did not tell any of her personal business. I did not even think about it.

✳ ✳ ✳

"I always take me wherever I go"

Oh, what we could be if we stopped carrying the remains of who we were.
—Tyler Knot Gregson

Although I don't know why, I did know early on that my mother, Inga, was different from any other mother living in the south in the 1960's. She did not speak like all the other mothers. Some people said she had a funny accent, and they could not understand her. I guess I was accustomed to her accent because I understood her perfectly well. The "th' sound was a challenge she never quite met, instead she used the "t" sound only. As an example, her directions were to, "Go take a bat." No, she did not want her two little blond daughters to go out and chase winged rodents. It was for us to go in the "bat(h)room," start the water in the "bat(h) tub" and clean ourselves from the sweat acquired playing outside in the heat soaked south.

There are letters in words that did not make a sound, so she asked, "Why were they in the word?" There was no "K" sound in knife. "The word is not *ka nife*—*it is nife*." To Inga, our phrases were the most confusing. "How can you go back and forth? You have to go forth before you go back to where you started." All these questions about language—we just spoke it. I did not bother to wonder the where and why of it all. My mom sure did. We were assigned a word of the week. A word printed on an index card was put on our placemat on the table on Monday mornings. My sister and I were required to look the word up to find the definition and use the word in sentences throughout the week. Although, we moaned and groaned about it the first few days, we came to look forward to the weekly activity and enjoyed flaunting our newly acquired vocabulary skills.

All the while, I was grumbling about having to do this silly thing that I did not want to do and asking out loud, "How is it going to help me anyway?" I had not realized that my mother spoke two languages fluently and four others well enough to communicate with others from those countries.

My mother thought differently. Perhaps it is why she escaped into her books to find solace with authors who thought more like she did. My grandfather, (Bobby's dad, Andrew, the truck driver) used to say to her, "Ingam, you got your wires crossed." I thought it was funny when I was a little girl but not so funny when I began to understand the meaning behind the saying.

It took a while to really comprehend that her being from another country had formed her thoughts. They were in no way, form, or fashion like any of the other mothers we met anywhere. Of course, others were raised in homes that provided them with a full belly, a warm bed and without fear of bombs being dropped on their heads. Neither they nor I had to worry if begging for food was a bad thing to do or had to attempt to erase the memory of seeing ourselves playing in the mirrored eyes of our dead infant brother. This is harsh but none the less, true. It certainly gives one an entirely different perspective on life and of people. It could be enough to drive one quite mad, or quite angry.

The women married to my dad's friends seemed nice, yet I cannot recall my mom going shopping or talking on the phone with any of them. My friends' mothers cooked and cleaned just like my mom. They took their children to church and my mother took us to the navy chapel regularly. My sister and I did not like it because we did not know any of the other children. We looked forward to the end when we were given cookies in a napkin. The closing song meant home was near and so was the time to strip off the itchy, starched cotton dresses and patent leather shoes that pinched our feet.

Inga did the tasks expected and then some. She took us to the symphony, leaning over to whisper the story behind the music. We went to the museum on days it rained. My sister, Selma always went straight for the exhibition of shrunken heads. Yes! There were actual shrunken human heads on display. Selma was sixteen months younger than I, yet she was a fearless being. She rushed right to the front of the glass display case, stopping with spine straight and hands on hips and glared with wide eyes, not even a blink, at the three shrunken heads each dangling from a string. I, on the other hand did not like this display at all but followed her because Mom wanted us to stay together. Great, right?!? I chose to peak from around the far end of the glass case whispering an insistent, "Let's *go*" Selma still stood as if she was messaging through some ancient telepathic method to the dead cored out heads that she was not afraid. She then would laugh and challenge me to come look, refusing to go one step further until I did.

It would be easier if they were fake. Each was only the size of a lemon, maybe even smaller. The eyes and mouth were sewn shut with some type of string or leather. They were tied with the excess dripping from the corners of the mouths, adding to the hideous nature. Selma, of course was not bothered one bit and questioned a museum volunteer. He assured us they were indeed real then proceeded to reveal the darken secrets of the procedure these poor rotten heads endured to become small so they could appear in this glass cubed space for all to view. I probably became two shades paler as he spoke. At some point, my ears protecting my brain started to ring to stop the piercing information from entering my mind. Pulling on Selma's clothes to indicate the urgent need to leave this spot prior to the floors opening up to swallow us into some tribal ritual hell. I was relieved when I felt us moving away in any direction than the one, we always started.

Yes, my mother wanted us to have experiences and learn. How shrunken heads fit into her plan of enlightenment is beyond my comprehension! Knowing my mom and the museum having a planetarium, her thoughts were more directed to the possibility of one of her girls being the first female astronaut.

Inga was not the type who liked to walk around history, satisfied to see what people generations prior were inspired to act upon or create. She felt a responsibility to act where there was injustice. She participated in the March of Dimes in our community. She always took fruit baskets to the custodians at our schools assuring we were standing by her as she said thank you for their work.

Inga had decided to keep her Norwegian citizenship status however she took part in American democracy. A true to life feminist, she marched in Washington for numerous causes (more than anyone I have ever known). She felt her participation was a benefit to those that came after her, her daughters, and granddaughters. She was entranced by the idea of American democracy. There too she was different, for her viewpoint had more a global sense not regionalized to one country. Yes, that also would cause more fire than smoke when you are living in the south and your mother identifies with the struggle of civil rights.

Another humiliation endured as a child certainly influenced the adult Inga. She was ridiculed for having high cheekbones and made to go to the back of the bus being bullied for being a "Laplander" (a slang word for the indigenous Sami people that inhabited the far northern parts of Norway). Her mother's family were Sami and raised reindeer. It is why the high cheekbones and why young Inga went to the back of the bus feeling shame and anger, although not sure what she had done to deserve such treatment.

***

Changing Our Corner of the World

The issue of judging people due to their race, ethnicity, sex or religious choice was taught to be unacceptable and could be dangerous. Inga would assuredly raise both her daughters' awareness. Awareness is not gained without exposure.

Inga determined her daughters would not be ignorant of the happenings of the world as well. She kept the magazines Time and Life on the coffee table in the living room. She did not push me or Selma to read them. The photos on the covers were enough to draw you to pick up the magazine and check it out. You read a story and see another interesting photo that leads you to read another story of a people or event somewhere in the world. Mom was always ready to answer questions or help you research for the answers.

Inga attempted to lead an authentic life full of beliefs on various issues. She strived to reflect her beliefs for her daughters to view. In doing so, she was demonstrating not just to be academics but to be active-making real differences in a changing world.

Inga met people and with a select few she would invest her time and engage in a relationship. From some I am sure she craved the intellectual stimulation from different points of view than those she was around frequently. Those closest to her generally accepted the status quo, did not read the newspaper, had not been students of history, and were not vested in the repercussions if the lessons were not learned and kept alive. Others she found interesting, she would introduce to her girls so they could hear their stories or know of the things they had seen. Why, you may ask, was this so important to Inga? She had this need for them to know there was so much out in the world that they could do and see. "Keep your options and your mind open. You can be anything you want to be."

Inga made friends with a local high school teacher who was married to a man that served on the school board. They had three children, the middle girl being the same age as myself. The family was African American. My mother, sister and I visited with them in their home in a nearby neighborhood a few times. I do not believe the sole purpose of this friendship was a learning experience for Selma and I. Inga made friends with many people. My dad however did not spend time visiting them.

The family was very nice and academic. The most striking difference was not that their skin color was darker, it was their father. He did not leave as soon as he ate dinner, rushing out the door so quickly that you could feel a breeze as the back door slammed. No, the dad was more like a dad you see on television, like Ward Cleaver on *Leave it to Beaver*. He would sit in his chair with his glasses on and read the paper. He would raise his head up every now and then to point out certain things he found interesting.

The girl the same age as me was named Deborah. My mother invited Deborah to join a community service group of girls meeting at a local church that she led once a week. We said a pledge to building character and taking care of the earth. The members wore uniforms and once a year had the opportunity to go to camp for a day. Each week we had different activities.

Inga had sent the group's enrollment list into the national office. Each member received a card identifying them as a member of the organization. The member's name, the date and the group number were listed on the front of the card. The pledge was listed on the back along with the organization emblem. It was exciting to be a card-carrying member and only being in elementary school. Well, all the girls received their cards except for Deborah.

Inga wrote letters and made long distance calls to come to an understanding of why she had not received the card for only one of the group's members. The organization suggested Inga send the enrollment list again. Inga was responsive and sent the required list not once or twice but three times. The last time was sent certified to assure the list had arrived at the correct destination. There were no more suggestions and there was not a member card either. A woman at the organization office had spoken with Inga on more than one occasion. Inga had become exasperated and somewhat bewildered as to why the member card for one child was repeatedly excluded. The woman explained the organization was not going to send a card for a black child.

Oh my! Inga became like a flame lit on a torch. She verified with the woman what she thought she heard she had said, then asked to speak to a supervisor. The answers became more evasive as she spoke to each supervisor willing to take the call transferred to them. Not one supervisor or authority in the organization confirmed the receptionist's pronouncement. Yet, not one agreed to send the membership card, only to say a card would not be given for the girl.

Inga, being totally incensed, wrote to the local newspaper exposing the injustice of the denial to send a membership card to the only girl in the group that happened to be black. Although I did not read the paper (well maybe the comics on Sundays only), it was not difficult to know that Inga's address in the paper received many responses. I heard her on the phone telling someone that a man had written for her to "Love America or leave it."

The phone started ringing at the house. It was Selma or I usually competing to answer the phone, no matter that it was rarely for us. The only phone in the house sat on the kitchen bar atop the phone book. Selma had scribbled alternate names for herself all over the phone book.

The unusual calls really did not make sense to Selma or me. We would just tell Mom what the message was like, "Don't like America, leave it. Get away from here. Move back from where you came from." The one that scared us all is when the caller said, "If you don't stop, we are going to burn a cross in your yard n_____ lover," click. Lucky me, I grabbed the phone on that message. Crying I ran to Mom, not knowing what all his threat entailed. I did not say the "N-word" because my sister and I knew we were not allowed to ever use that word. I grew up thinking that was the worst word ever muttered by anyone anywhere.

I recall we turned off the lights and got down face first on the floor in the hallway when a truck came down the road that night of the threat. Someone from a truck yelled the word we were not allowed to say and a string of other profane words. My mom kept her hands on my and Selma's back speaking quietly and telling us to not move. My dad was not there at the time of the incident. He had left for the race car shop. The drive by threat was frightening enough, I cannot imagine the trauma of a burning cross left in the yard or bricks thrown in the windows of your house would create.

These were early behavioral modification tactics by those who had no idea of what those meant, all they knew and knew it all too well, is fear will shut people up if they are not agreeing with you. My mom was not the kind to hush up until she had rectified a wrong or was sure she had made her point. I believe she thought some were incapable of getting past themselves to come to an understanding about the ugly power of hate. Perhaps, they did, and it drove them to hateful actions. I tend to think they really did not think too much about it. They just acted the way those around them and/or those that raised them. The thought processes needed to overcome actions of bigotry required either a more simplistic or higher-level capacity.

I do not know if the membership card was ever received. I do not know my dad's

response to the situation, if he was angry at my mother, the threatening caller or the people driving the truck screaming at us. It was never mentioned again.

We did not return for another year of the organization's local group meetings. The pledge had some very, nice words but was not truly practiced with all people. Inga would have declined to have been involved in such an organization. Not a woman with her experiences when the whole world was threatened by a group of people with a similar mind set.

***

Charleston — 1974

Our Lefler family life seemed to go along well enough. We had a good place to live with a lot of friends. Our family went to the races together and participated in other activities with our race family. We spent holidays with my dad's family in North Carolina. Dad had not been out to sea in a long time.

The summer of 1974, I was thirteen years old. I liked riding my bike and singing along with my battery-operated radio. The bike ride often headed toward the neighborhood boat landing with access to the Ashley River. It was peaceful watching the water change from a calm stillness to waves formed by the wakes of the boats going by. Just standing there holding the bike up between my legs waiting on the water to arrive lapping near my feet. The sounds of birds signaling one another, the croaking of frogs and the quiet scattering of fiddler crabs, added to the natural sound of summer.

At some time, dad and I had developed a routine of watching, *The Wonderful World of Disney*, at seven o'clock every Sunday. I did not miss it even if it was a rerun or one of the animal documentaries that I did not really like. Dad would gather the saltines, a butter knife for spreading peanut butter as he settled in his recliner, and I was on the floor in front of the television. It was my job to pop the tops of a *Coca-Cola*, in the six and half ounce glass bottles before the *Tinkerbell* darted across the top of the castle. It was the signal the show was ready to begin. We had enjoyable small talk during this time, odd but welcomed by both of us.

MY MOTHER'S SUITCASE

When the show was over it was not unusual to be told to go and fetch my daddy's cigarettes from the cab of his truck. Heck, I had been sent to the corner store when I was even younger with a note written by daddy and the money to buy a pack of *Winstons*.

This particular search would alter life as I had come to know it. I noticed my daddy's handwriting on a stamped letter addressed to a Miss Evette Falls of Atlanta, Georgia as it fell from the driver's visor. I placed it back above from where it fell while I continued to search for the red and white pack of smokes. I grabbed them and took the opened pack to the Chief as he laid back in his lazy boy recliner. He was only stretched out on that recliner on Sundays, for if it was any other day he would be working or at the race car shop a few miles away at his friend's house.

I did not think anything about that letter until weeks later. My dad and sister had gone to visit my dad's family in North Carolina. I am not sure why mom and I stayed home but I had plans to catch the bus to go roller skating with my friends.

Come to think of it, I do not ever remember my sister going to the roller rink. That was probably another reason I loved going, to have something apart from her. Selma was the room when she was in it. There was not enough spotlight for anyone else. She was bold, incredibly smart, and very pretty. Whatever "It" was, well, my baby sister had "It" and then some. She was a daddy's girl. He did not seem to swat her away. He seemed to enjoy her tagging along to the race car shop. If I ever asked to go, he chose to flip a coin. Somehow, she won the coin toss most of the time and off they'd go.

Selma and dad being in North Carolina left me with drying the dishes that mom was washing. There was a buzz of excitement for it was skate night. My skates were sitting beside the front door with the laces tied together so with one swoop I could be out the door and down to the corner to catch the bus. My mom pried and asked why I was so happy? Perhaps a boy I planned to meet and skate with? She even said the name of the one boy that I indeed would want to hold hands and skate with when it is couple skate time. (The lights would be lowered, the music slowed and the announcer in a deep voice spoke into the microphone, "It is now time for The Couple's Skate.") Of course, I denied it because it was my mom asking. No one wants to admit, out loud to their mom that they liked a boy. She asked again, all the time knowing, and we laughed as I placed the last dry dish in its appointed place in the cabinet. I then teasingly said, "Well, Daddy has a letter in his truck for Evette Falls!" All sudden, the laughing stopped, the color in my mom's face drained away. She stood frozen, shoulders slightly forward with her arms folded across her stomach as if she were about to throw up. I asked if she was all right. Her breathing became faster, and tears fell. I tried to erase what I had said, making excuses that perhaps it was someone in the navy, but mom just shook her head no. The name was not familiar to me, but it was quite evident that it was well known to my mother.

Inga then pronounced she was going to North Carolina. "When? Now?" I asked. Mom was heading for answers and packing a suitcase was the only brake. I was given the option to go with her or stay with a friend. I had looked forward all week to going skating and was not going to change that now. Luckily, I found someone to stay with before my mom left. I would find out how lucky I was to not have witnessed our family dissolve as my sister did at my grandmother's house.

***

How quickly things can change. Although I did not realize at the time, my childhood came to a screeching halt once mother, with my sister in tow, returned on Sunday from North Carolina. The illusion of our family vaporized as though we had not ever been a family--not a real family anyway. No amount of pleading, begging, fit throwing, or fairy dust was going to revive whatever our gathering and traveling together had been for fourteen years.

Selma, not known to possess warm and fuzzy feelings for anything other than creatures with four legs, was rattled from what she witnessed at our grandmother's house. It was she who told me that our parents were going to divorce. There was no sit down in the living or around the dining room table for a family meeting to say, "Your mom and I are going to divorce. Although we may not love each other anymore, we will always love you both. Our plans are....." Yeah, that did not occur. From that time on if our parents were in close range of one another, there was a scene for all around to view. Screaming, cussing, crying and all perpetrated by my mother. If she really thought about it, causing a scene challenging my father's inflated need to be proud would backfire causing him to push away--not attempt to fix it like a race car that could not start.

My mother revealed she had one ally in my dad's family. She spilled that fact to someone on the other end of the phone during one of her late night, drunk calling episodes. She reported, Aunt Inez was against a divorce because of the girls. Mom filled in; Bobby was close to his mother. His mother admitted that she knew all these years about Bobby and his girlfriend still seeing and writing each other during his entire marriage.

My sister and I being in bed right down the hall heard too much about our parent's marriage during that *one* call. I believe my mother in her stupor purposely raised her slurred voice so that we would hear the specifics. Mom went on to divulge that went she went to confront Bobby about the letter found in his truck when she encountered his mother, Margaret. His mother that told her that Bobby had let her know of all her (Inga's) affairs with men since Bobby and she married. His mother knew of the affair she had in Japan. Bobby also told his mother of an affair during the days we spent at the house across from Aunt Inez during one of dad's long deployments after returning to the states. The relationship had resulted in an unwanted pregnancy. Margaret said she had known about that one and told her son herself.

The pregnancy did not go to term. The details still shielded from complete disclosure due to protecting someone else in the family. That one uncovered secret explained all the fuss of the damn stove. In probability the angst over the stove was not about the money spent, who bought the stove or my sister being name after my aunt instead of my grandmother. It was more to do with the immigrant wife having an affair when the native son was away serving his country.

Inga boasted of flirting with a man while in Annapolis saying that almost ended the marriage then, but because of *the girls, emphasized purposefully,* he stayed.

Selma and I looked at each other, not knowing what to say. Selma undoubtedly had heard this play out firsthand, in North Carolina at our grandmother's house when mom went to confront dad.

There were more nights and more calls. My first thoughts were, she had waited until Selma and I were asleep to make these calls. It became clear why she called late at night. She placed those calls when she was drunk. I do not know all the people she called. I know she called my dad and would cry. Once she begged that she could be *their* maid (*Dad and the old/new girlfriend*). I felt angry at mom for saying that and dad for putting her in a place to say such things. The crying seemed to never cease. I had come to a point when I just wished she would stop the crying and do something else, anything else. The crying did not stop.

***

Inga's crying soon turned into rage fueled by alcohol. I never had seen my mom drink, although once she was sick—more like hung over—after an oyster roast, she and dad had gone to at a nearby beach. Dad had me help him pour out all the beer from the refrigerator the next morning. I am not saying she had a problem with drinking, just that I had not seen her drink, nor had I seen her drunk until dad moved out of the rented house and to housing on the base. I did not know where he was staying but Selma had been there. Mom would drive her over to the base and have Selma go to ask dad to come down to the car to talk to mom. Of course, dad would not come to the car, but mom would want Sis to go back to plead with him to come down to the car.

***

A Boozing Bazaar in the Woods

My mother seemed more at home with other people at their houses then she was at our house, (if that makes any sense at all.) Inga was animated when talking and exchanging ideas with the few friends she had, or new acquaintances met out while shopping or visiting local sights. She was engaging and appeared happy.

There was not much opportunity for her to interact with another adult at our house. Dad historically, had not been home. The only time I knew they spent together, in company of one another, was on Sunday afternoons. The bedroom door was locked and if it was knocked on, the reply was they were *taking a nap*. A directive had been given, "To go outside." No talk was heard about the books my mom had read or thoughts of current events. A slight possibility of a nap occurred. It was a more likely they were participating in what brought them together in the first place and it was not dancing.

So many available reasons of why my mother started to drink alcohol--loneliness and boredom just two contenders. Do not forget to toss in the genetic factor or post traumatic stress of a childhood spent in a war zone. Add the fact she had discovered her husband was writing letters to the girlfriend he had known most of his life. The *one* he left behind when he joined the navy. The *one* he knew before marrying her. The *one*, the wedding ring worn by Inga was intended to be placed on *the one's left* hand.

* * *

The opportunity to see my mother intoxicated occurred at a neighbor's house directly across the street. They had not lived in the house very long. Inga, the man, and woman became fast drinking buddies. I did not know she had met them until I was looking for her one afternoon. I walked outside and could hear her talking and laughing. I followed the sound and located her visiting in the back yard. These were not the usual people she sought out to discuss what she viewed on the evening news or a recent editorial in the newspaper.

I popped around the side of the neighbor's house greeted to, "Come on back", by the couple. An accurate account of what I saw in a backyard would be best described as a roadside circus. The setting wiped out the reason I went to speak to my mother.

The three adults were sitting in the foldable aluminum chairs with the plastic webbing weaved to form the bottom and back of the chairs. The square head of the man looked like a child's building block sitting on top of shoulders, without benefit of a neck. His mouth, losing shape without his dentures, formed a drawstring pouch slightly open to guzzle the beer in the can that he clutched in his right hand. His top half was a crisp apple red. In contrast were his stick legs, knotted at the knees, which stuck out from worn shorts with a pressed crease. They were as white as his bleached thin t-shirt. He leaned back in his chair balancing it on the back leg much like the cigarette stuck to the bottom of his lip—not falling even while he laughed.

A side act was near the picnic table. A lanky woman with stringy bright yellow hair dressed in a terrycloth, aqua colored romper. The chipped red nail polish on her toes was easily seen as she wore thin worn flip flops. Coaxing her three-year old daughter in baby talk to come to her, "Don't you want mama to give you a sip of beer? Come to mama." Reaching out like a contortionist beckoning the little girl to come place her mouth on the side of a plastic cup. Slowly, the tiny blue eyed blond girl with a pony-tail on the top of her head, much like a shih tzu puppy, flopping up and down with every movement came toward her trainer/mom. Her mother tilted the cup and the little girl pulled back shaking her head side to side while spitting out whatever she had sipped making sounds and saying it was yucky. Clearly, this had not been the first time as the mother reminded the others how the child had gotten so stupefied a day ago that she could not stand up. Recalling she had poured it in the favored sippy cup.

My mother serving as the only member of the audience, exploded with laughter, and clapped for the performance. Yep, a behavior my mother would have abhorred a short time prior, she was condoning with her laughter.

A Slow Burn Led to a Combustion

Unfortunately, laughing was not my mother's usual reaction to having a snoot full. Her speech was slurred. Her unsteady gait swaying side to side. A wall was necessary to avoid her from collapsing to the floor. She looked like a human bumper car bouncing from one wall to another.

It did not matter the time of day or night; my sister and I were always on high alert. One day, relieved to not see her car when we came home from school, we went around the side of the garage heading to the back door, hoping it was not locked. As I turned the doorknob able to push it open into the garage. I viewed the steps leading into the house. Just three brick steps, yet that day they were littered with glass, pieces of photos and strips of material. A pair of scissors lay next to the mess. They had been dropped there when the destruction was completed. Noticing it was photos of my father, I instinctively shoved my sister back out of the garage door and locked it so she could not come in.

Selma banged on the glass panel of the door asking, "What is it? Why can I not come in?" Not shouting back, I stood at the door looking into her eyes and said, "You do not need to see this. Let me clean it up and then I will let you in." No yelling, no squabbling or continuing to bang on the door, Selma's eyes filled with tears while her head dropped, nodding yes as she turned to the side of the garage.

Breaching the steps ever so carefully but still hearing the grinding as I stepped on pieces of glass, I opened the back door leading into the kitchen, grabbed a paper bag (the days before the choice of paper or plastic) along with the broom and dustpan, turned back around to start the process of cleaning up what I discovered was the remains of photos of my dad now cut up into several pieces. I started with what was left of the torn and twisted frames, then the bigger pieces of glass, concerned they may tear the bag as they slipped past the sides to the bottom of the bag. The larger pieces made more of a thud. The smaller pieces had a higher pitched sound, almost musical when the shards swept into the dustpan were dumped in with the bigger pieces. Those sounds and views were distracting, a much easier task then using my index finger and thumb to pick up the photos and bits of material to one of my dad's favorite shirts, (the buttons still hanging all in one strip).

Thinking all of this had gone too far, this was very serious. This was my daddy all cut up, my daddy! My mother had taken his pictures down off the walls, ripped them out of the frames, cutting them up in a place where she knew her daughters would see them. What have we done? It was not our fault. We were turned inside out too.

My scalp began to sizzle like a road after the rain on a hot summer day in the south, as it was too much to take in. I had come to know how to turn my feelings on and off, like using the spigot for the garden hose. No alcohol, cigarettes, weed required for me. I had now learned the chill needed to numb me.

Once all was swept up, I opened the door to the garage calling for Selma to come on in. I held the paper bag in my other hand, stepping out on the concrete to go and place the bag in the garbage can. Nothing in the bag could be glued or taped together, kind of like the lives we had now, torn into shreds and no longer recognized as ours.

Selma wanted to see what had been on the steps, what was in the bag. I was not much older than she was and although she might be able to stare down ancient shrunken heads—seeing her daddy all cut up would have been a sight she could not erase. What was my mother thinking when she left the mess for not just her daughters, (we were also his daughters) to look at? I guess she knew how to become numb, but hers took alcohol. Sadly, I did not think she could turn off the tap.

Unfortunate as it was to see the mess left on the back doorsteps, it was not to be the end of the anger. It was pure bliss to arrive home from school and the black Gran Prix with red pinstriping not to be parked in the garage. We would fix our own dinner, watch TV, and head off to bed. Lying awake waiting for a parent, (either one) to come home was a bit unnerving. My bed was the closet one to see the road. We had opened the window so we could listen for a car or truck pull up in the drive. Headlights were a part of our game, "Does any parent care to come home because we are scared out of our wits?" Most often we fell off to sleep before anyone was home.

***

Running through the Woods

On a night to be remembered, Selma and I noticed the headlights crest over our bedroom ceiling. A quick look out the window confirmed mom was home. We scooted under our covers pretending to be asleep. The alarm clock was soon heading down the hall calling our names. There she was, "*The queen of the neighborhood bar*", sloshing her way toward our room. Stopping at our door with the hall light on, all we could see was her outline. She had her hands above her head holding unto the door, hip shifted to one side, slurring her words, peppered in the profanity. Selma's and my name mixed in all the jumble. We did not understand how we were to respond. She turned and used the walls to guide herself to her room.

We were premature to be relieved, for in a matter of minutes she had returned. She came in our room wearing her robe and began slinging a belt at both of our beds. There was no target; our heads, torso, or legs, wherever the belt landed. We pulled our covers up over our heads while screaming for her to stop.

She left and I quickly went and locked the door. My sister shoved her twin bed up to the door. I placed my hip on the other side of the dresser, sliding it to help block the door. Inga returned beating on the door and cussing us for locking her out. The doorknob was being shook which rattled the items on our dresser. She called each of our names along with choice words usually associated with drunks in barroom fights.

Well, this was not a barroom, and Selma and I sure were not going to fight. Going over to my bed, I hopped on it, scooting close to the window it was under. I loosened the tabs that held the screen in and pushed it out to fall in the shrubs out front, and instructed Sis, "Come on. Get out the window." I tried my best not to let my nerves get the better of me by being too loud so that the monster at the door could not hear.

Selma did not hesitate. She came on my bed, up to the window headfirst, turning her body around hanging on the frame with her fingertips. I grasped her forearms sliding to her wrists to lower her down to the ground. I told her to *run*, whispering I would try to meet up with her. That was as much of a plan as we had to prepare.

The hurricane had arrived. We had a moment to take cover. The door was rattling from the banging of fists and kicking but the lock was holding. The screaming, laced with profanity persisted. The shattering of glass was heard. It was our school photos which were thrown and then the frames being bent along with our faces, as they were kicked under the bedroom door.

No time to waste before the fire breathing dragon burst through the door. I hopped up on the window frame and looked out. One of the next-door boys—David—held his bike up against the brick wall of the house so the seat could be easily met with my foot as I slid down the wall. He helped me down to level ground and said he would keep a watch out, "*Just run.*"

Barefoot and in my pajamas, I took off down the asphalt street. David whistled and I knew he was warning me to get out of sight. I ran across the main street in our neighborhood up through my sister's friend's yard to dive behind the bushes that lined the side of the house. I was breathing so hard I was concerned the sound would somehow give my hiding space away. Slowing the pace of my breathing seemed to hurt from my heart ramming my chest wall.

Every sense heightened due to the fear of what was going to happen next. "Oh no, it can't be! Please God help me," I thought seeing headlights coming from our road. The car rolled to a stop causing my heartbeat to speed up again to the point I felt I was going to throw up. It was the black Gran Prix turning right in front of me going toward the entrance of our neighborhood.

David whistled and I felt it safe to briefly emerge from the hedges. I asked where Selma was. He was not sure but offered to find out, arranging to meet up with me as soon as he could find out.

A barefoot run through yards and up the next road, stubbing my big toe, caused me to limp up to my best friend's house. I knew they were off on a family vacation across the US. It is the only place I knew to find solace like I had so many times before for similar reasons.

I waited for what seemed like forever, partly because I was dodging headlights in the shadows of their house. What a relief to hear David's whistle. Stepping out of the shadows I waved at him. He braked and slowed as he approached me and relayed the location of my sister. She was at the campfire with Rusty and a few others. They had campfires every Friday night unless it was raining. David added that she was going to hang out there assuring me she was safe. He, his brother Tommy, and Rusty would keep watch on her and our house.

My neighbor who loved to open the back yard gate to let our Pekingese just to laugh as I would chase after it, really came through that night.

It was time to see if I could find a place to hide for a little while. The garage door at my best friend's house was heavy. I struggled to raise it just enough to get inside, checked the back door hoping it was open, but—Nope— no key under the mat or any other place I could think to look for it. Finally, for some odd reason, I climbed on top of the washer and dryer, rolled up a rag towel for a pillow, and pulled up the rug from the top of the dryer for a blanket.

I woke up early, only to recall what had happened just hours before. I was only thirteen, but all my muscles hurt. I was "ouing" and "owwing" with every movement. My head felt like a hammer had knocked in nails all night through my eyeballs! Yuk. I scooted out the garage door, the way I came in.

The dew was cold and soothed my swollen feet. The sun was barely up. Unsure of where to go, I headed to the rented white brick house on Ventura Drive. Oh, how I wished David (next door neighbor), would ride up on his ten speed and give me a ride home on his handlebars. No such luck. My poor bare feet took to the asphalt to cross the street. Why did I cross the street? Simply there was nowhere else to go. My heart revved up as I crossed each neighbor's yard leading me closer to the white brick house.

Whew, what a relief as the view of the drive showed no black Gran Prix—hopefully the garage was empty as well. The gate was locked. The back door to the garage was closed. I carefully tip toed to peek in the door for the car I had come to fear. Yay, no car! My head dropped as I headed in the back door. Selma, with the benefit of the boys on lookout, had made it home before I did and was asleep in her bed.

There on the floor right outside our door was our school pictures that had been torn from the wall. A display of broken objects such as glass shards, bent frames and many small pieces of what had once been pictures of my sister and me. In one photo, Selma had her hair braided to the side in a ponytail a wore her Norwegian sweater. She easily looked like she could be a schoolgirl from Norway with high cheek bones and creamy skin.

I was not to upset about one of my pictures being ruined, you sure could not tape these together no matter how well a puzzle piece fitter you were. In this one picture I had insisted on wearing a dress that my cousin had given me despite my mother's objections. It was too big and made of green checkerboard fabric. A silly grin on my face had me looking like a frog ready to jump to the next lily pad.

***

MY MOTHER'S SUITCASE

SELMA INEZ LEFLER

SCHOOL PHOTO IN HER NORWEGIAN SWEATER

I must admit I felt the ice pick running cold through my heart to see what our mother had done to the photos of the two little girls she always wanted. I guess that meant she did not want us anymore. The whisk broom and dustpan swept up more family to be dumped in a brown paper grocery bag. The shards tended to stick in between the boards of the wood floor. I cut myself, prying one loose so there was yet another mess to clean up. I had no tears. I did not have anyone to help me to place a band-aid on my cut. My mother was not going to say, "Poor baby", then kiss the top of my head. I knew those days were gone. Sad, when you realize something is over before it was time to be over.

Finally, with stuff put away as it could be, considering the incident that happened the night before, I closed the door to the room my sister and I shared and locked the door. It did not matter that we were sharing the same room now. It helped to have someone aid you in blocking the door and sliding out the window.

My bed did not care that I had a dirty nightgown and filthy feet when I slumped down upon it. The next thing I heard was my dad's voice calling our names as he was walking down the hall. Startled, dad reached our doorknob before Sis or I had placed our feet on the floor. His tone was not as demanding as expected. Selma opened the door.

It was clear that things were not as squared away as usual with Selma's bed cocked sideways up close to the door. The screen was off the half-opened window and the curtains were hanging in and out on the windowsill. Yep, things were out of place. I did not know how Selma felt but I was too overwhelmed to be frightened what the Chief had to say about the state of our room.

Dad shook his head side to side then asked if we had eaten breakfast. I noticed he looked to where our pictures had been displayed, rubbing his thumb across an indention in the wall.

The tension still felt, like being on a carnival ride. You are stuck sideways, squishing your friend against the side, but before the ride slings you, and then your friend is now squishing you. If it had been mom in the house, I know we would have felt like the roller coaster had jumped the track from the highest peak and Selma and I were sent sailing in the sky.

Dad took out the bowls and spoons. He asked if the Cheerios were okay to have for breakfast? I knew this was bad because he never had done this before, ever.

Dad looked around the house while Sis and I took a bath and changed our clothes. He sat down in his recliner but kept it in the upright position. He waited. Odd, he was not trying to rush out the door. He called out, "Wanda and Selma, come on in here. I need to talk to you." Wrapping a towel around my wet hair, I followed Selma to the couch.

Come to find out, one of the neighbors had somehow called dad and told him there had been trouble going on in the house last night. I'm not sure if we were just too tired physically or not willing to relive the previous night's events, not a sound was uttered. Nor did we raise our heads as we were perched on the edge of the couch that had come with us all the way from Japan.

He informed us things were going to change from that point on. He revealed his plans starting with him moving back in the house. No one would need to climb out the windows anymore. There would be someone at the house when we got home from school. Selma and I both jerked and looked at him with what dad correctly identified as fear. He quickly responded, "I do not know who it is going to be yet. It may be me until I find someone. It will not be your mom. Do you understand?" I could see Sis nod her head yes and I did as well. I knew he could be demanding but the need to slam the bed and dresser against our bedroom door would not be necessary.

* * *

The next day, just as dad had said, he was at the house when we got home from school. He then told us Ella would be at the house each day when we came home from school. "Ella, isn't she Mom's friend?" He went on explaining she had called and offered to help, and he felt it was going to be ok. Continuing, that he would be home in a couple of hours after. It would not be long.

It was not that I did not like Ella. She was older than Mom and was also, from Norway. Mom searched out others from her homeland to talk her native language. We had been to Ella's large house before with mom. She was not a drinking buddy unless you count tea. Ella read the tea leaves. It was a method of telling your future. Hey, it did not cause me any problems so—whatever. Ella also used a deck of specialized cards to foretell your life events. There were odd looking detailed characters on those cards.

Again, I did not understand, but no one was tearing up photos or screaming profanity at me or Sis so I did not protest. No crying or banging on doors was happening, so she could come and sit at our dining room table and flip those cards around all she wanted until dad drove up.

The fact that I and Selma somehow managed to keep our grades up during this time was a magic trick, maybe not so much for Selma because the only grade she had was an A. Me? I was an honor roll student but unlike my brilliant sister I had to work for every single point. To tell the truth, she is the reason why I worked so hard. I wanted my dad to praise me at the dinner table like he did her when it was report card time.

I personally would have preferred to live at school then ever go home. I loved being in high school with all the games, dances, the friends without the distraction of home. Although, boarding the bus, a new tune greeted Selma and I, "Crazy Lady, Crazy Lady." A credit due to my mother's neighborhood antics. We should have bowed and clapped instead of silently sliding over to our seats. I never had felt shame as I did, just riding the bus to school.

At least, things had calmed down at home. Ella was always there after school asking us how our day went. Dad came home and had dinner with us. Occasionally, he asked Ella to stay a little longer so he could go to the race car shop. He would be back by 8 p.m. so we did not have to watch for headlights on the ceiling of our room. The jitteriness was still there but not as much as when the dragon was burning down our door.

I did not talk much to Ella, but she sure liked to talk to my dad. The topic was almost always about my mother. Things Inga had said to Ella as a friend, her friend was now sharing with Bobby. I was just a kid and knew this was a betrayal.

Although, I was scared sick of what my mother had become, I did not like someone telling her secrets. You do not need to be an adult to recognize it as wrong. What did Ella expect to gain for her deeds? Surely, she did not see her and Bobby in those cards or tea leaves?

Every Circus
Needs a Clown

A few weeks had gone by. We were back into our routine of being young teens. It was not Ella who met us one afternoon. It was Dad's pick up in the drive. Well, okay maybe he was off early. That idea shattered when we entered the living room, and he was sitting up in his recliner with his uniform on and he asked his daughters to have a seat that he had something to tell us.

Oh my, as my heart started to race, what now? Dad went on to tell Selma and I that our mother was found in her car at the Isle of Palms beach. The police had a hard time waking her. An ambulance was called and took her to a hospital downtown. The doctors say she is going to be ok. They do want to keep her for a few days. Bobby also said one of the doctors asked to speak to Selma and me. He would pick us up from school tomorrow and take us to the appointment.

The Chief was there to pick us up right on time. We took the interstate to downtown so that meant she was not in the naval hospital. We parked but still had a long walk before entering a large building. Large double glass doors held open by the Chief led us into a lobby area. Some people were sitting and others standing in a nearby lobby area. Bobby walked right past them heading toward the elevator.

There was no mistaking, he knew where he was going so my guess was that he had been here a time or two.

We entered the dingy, stuffy smelling elevator with Selma presenting herself right in front of the elevator buttons. She waited for dad to tell her which floor we were going to, then pressed the large round button with bright white numbers stamped on them. Once completed, she turned to dad beaming as if she had just won a gold medal in the Olympics of elevator button pushing. He patted her on the shoulders as she turned around to face the elevator doors. Selma looked at me with a smile and I did not think she was so brilliant to be smiling at a time like this. We were riding up in this contraption to go see a doctor that shrinks heads. Maybe not like those ugly shrunken heads on display at the museum, yet here we are to speak to him about something I am sure neither she nor I want pulled out of our heads.

It was only the three of us riding up to someplace. The elevator dinged as we reached and past each floor. I had not counted or noticed what floor dad had said we were going. Nope, I was attempting to not touch anything or let anything touch me. The mirrored glass on the back wall of this box had many fingers and handprints all over it. A tattletale sign that either there had been a whole lot of people riding in this box today or that no one cares to clean it. Odd, how you tend to take on the compulsiveness of others, like Dad with, "Get your hands off the car windows. I just cleaned the car." I understand the command, now looking at the different sizes of the handprints. Adult size could be seen too. You'd think they would know better. Thank goodness the elevator dinged, and the doors opened for us to exit.

Time to change from the "Mr. Clean" channel to "What's Up Bobby?" Bobby walked up to the desk and said something to the lady sitting behind it. Sis looked at me, no longer smiling and shrugged her shoulders. Dad had us all sit down on a padded bench near a large window that looked out over the parking lot where we had walked a country mile from to get in the building. It did not seem so far looking down from the window. There were windows on the other side behind the lady at the desk—long hallways on each side of her with windows only on our side. The other side had many doors with numbers below some sort of name.

I was seated on one side and Selma on the other of our dad. My hands were folded in my lap and feet dangling because my feet did not reach the floor. Selma had spotted the truck and was pointing out to dad where it was parked. He shook his head as he looked straight ahead to the wall ahead as if he had a bead on a target.

Selma then tapped my knee, and I looked the direction she pointed, nodding that yes I could see it--when I really had not. She plopped down beside dad and started swinging her feet. He reached out and patted her on her left knee as if to calm her without a word. I was not familiar with this dad that did not look at his watch or blow a gasket when we were doing something that aggravated him. This started my head buzzing with all kinds of thoughts, "Were Selma and I going to be locked up in this hospital? What are we not being told? Is someone going to take us away and I will not be able to see my friends or go to my school again?" The woman had said something to dad, and he stood up. I had not heard this and was seated as my heart was pounding, fearful for what was to come next.

A numbness grabbed a hold of me, and my body seemed to float as I followed Bobby into an office. He told Selma and I to sit down and the doctor will be there in a few minutes, then left the office. I sat there next to my sister, neither one able to touch the floor with our feet. No words were exchanged.

This room was larger, maybe three to four times larger than any doctor's office I had ever been in. It was larger than the dentist with all the equipment they have as well. There was not a large reclining chair or flat exam table to sit on. I did not see any stethoscopes anywhere. There was a large window, like the ones on the other side of the hall. Bookcases lined the wall behind the desk and behind where Selma and I were sitting. There was a small table with a couple of chairs with black padded seats in the corner adjacent to the wall that had the door and light switch on it.

A coffee cup, pencil and a pad sat on the table along with a small stack of books. "So many books in this room," I thought. This doctor must like to read as much as mom does.

Then, just as the Chief said, the door opened allowing a streak of sunlight to cross the floor from one of the windows on the other side of the hall. A man with a white coat walked in the room. When he closed the door, the sunshine disappeared only to be seen under the small crack under the door. I am not a patient battling their demons, but it was as if hope slipped out of the room with the sunshine. I'm just mentioning this in case someone needs some hope to hang around and not disappear. The good doctor may need to think about that symbolism. I would have thought he may have thought of it already! OK, need to calm down now.

The man in the white coat with long arms and legs was mesmerized by what he was reading. He did not look up or stop perusing as he stepped behind the large desk. There were stacks of similar folders piled on both sides of his calendar which was centered to the edge on his desk.

The reading man, I presumed was a doctor, sat down in the high back chair. I was certain he did not have the disadvantage of his feet not being able to touch the floor as tall as he was. He placed his elbows on the desk, leaned forward barely looking up from the chart he had opened in front of him. The folder must have contained some important or interesting information for a grown man to be so rude as to not look up and at least say hello when he entered a room. Perhaps he did not know we were there or knew and because we were children, he did not think he had to be polite.

His hair was reddish and shaped like a clown's, fluffy and round. There was a bow tie sitting at his neck. I never had seen a bow tie before. I bet if I could see under the desk his shoes were probably three times too big and some off color.

He must have completed his reading, or he finally noticed Selma and I were present. He looked up, closed the folder, and told us he was a psychiatrist.

He asked us if we understood what kind of a doctor he was. We both shook our heads, "No." The doctor gave some sort of answer. It was difficult to listen, trying to understand why we were in a room at a hospital with a head (shrinking) doctor that looked like a clown. Thoughts were flying in my mind like;—"Is my mother here?"—"Am I going to have to see her?"—"Are they going to bring her in here?"—"I do not want to see her"—"Do you think Selma and I are crazy too?" and "Are going to lock us up in this hospital?"

Wait, he just asked us what? "What are our feelings about our mother trying to kill herself?" Wait! What? Then he proceeded to ask how we felt about our parents getting a divorce. He saw shrugged shoulders from both of us. He continued being intrusive with his inquires. Although I do not know why he bothered. After all, he had more information about what was happening in our family then either one of us knew. "Did we want to live with, our mother or our father?" he asked. This one, we had covered. I answered as Selma did, "My dad." He requested we give him a reason why. The answer was easy, "Because we want to."

The final inquiry from Doctor Man was, "Wanda, are you all right?" "Selma, are you all right?" The response was, "Yes," from the two of us. Then, up and out of the chairs the girls of Bobby and Inga went to the lobby where dad was sitting on the same padded bench with his elbows on his knees, his right-hand picking at a fingernail on his left hand. His ice crystal blue eyes were looking straight ahead. Was this how my dad looked when he was nervous? It was the closest I had ever seen him looking concerned, almost like he was waiting outside the principal's office caught for streaking down the hall. We exchanged places as we sat on the padded bench and Bobby went in to talk or listen to the head shrink. He was not in there more than five minutes. He should not have been, for there was not much to tell of our get-together with the good doctor.

It is odd, we sisters did not talk about what we had just heard. Nor did we talk about the chaos, the crazy beatings, what happened in North Carolina, or the looming cloud of our parent's divorce. Surprisingly enough, we did not even push each other's buttons. I guess it was not fun anymore. Plus, we were being dinged like elevator buttons enough anyway.

Selma could be so annoying and if any one person could push my buttons it was her. If I liked any boy she would go after them. They would turn their limited attention span to her and then she would drop them and move on to another.

Her table manners left something to be desired. I had always been a picky eater and listening to her smack her food drove me straight up a wall. I would stand up a cereal box between us at the table and she moved it. She continued to smack her food with her mouth open. The worst part is I would look at her and she would stick out her tongue, full of chewed up food. Sis would laugh and I would fume. I cannot believe I even missed that gross event.

Selma was still in elementary school, and I went to high school. There were no middle schools during our scholastic glory days. The weekends I hung out with my friends with skating and sleepovers. Selma went with dad to the race car shop and would sleep over at the house where the shop was located. She had become good friends with the daughter of dad's racing buddy. So, the split was not intentional, but it happened, nonetheless. What sisterhood feelings, we may have had, wilted away like a vase full of forgotten wildflowers. No wonder when we needed one another to bounce feelings off, we did not, because it was hard to put into words. We no longer had access to just sit and talk. She and I were the only ones that had been swimming in this murky pool of adult nonsense. At least the only two with no say and a high risk of drowning.

Sis and I continued to tread water. Waving and smiling for those looking into the cesspool of our once care-free childhoods. Our lives continued with going to school, coming home to Ella, Daddy punching in at home on the dot. Routine returned. No more crazy lady calls when we boarded the bus. Life was better.

Can't Deny it, if You Write it

Ella kept compulsively flipping her character cards and speaking to Bobby like they were dear, dear friends. One evening she started chatting away. Bob had evidently asked for her assistance about going to court with Inga and needed some type of evidence about the state of her mental health. Ella thought for a moment then you could see a light bulb go off. She smiled and started speaking so fast in Norwegian.

Bobby stood beside the kitchen table looking at her like I had seen him look at my mother when he was becoming annoyed. I happened to be watching all of this transpire from the kitchen sink. Ella then looked and asked me where the little green suitcase of my mother's was kept. I said to her, "I do not know." Ella, now attempted to describe the suitcase filled with Inga's writings. "Wanda, you know, the small green one that is hard to lock the latches?" she tried to hook me in again.

I began to walk out of the dining room, ignoring Ella's trying to drag me into her betrayal. Stopped by the Chief before reaching the door, I was trapped and I knew it, as did my stomach, clenching into a knot. My dad, the man who had offered stability in this storm which also blew the winds that started the waves to surge, looked in my eyes and asked if I knew where this suitcase was. I answered, "Yes." I heard Ella huff and suck in her teeth in irritation.

Dad asked me to show him where the suitcase was located. I led him down the hall to the guest bedroom and pointed at the top of the left closet door. You would have thought the Chief had found a pot of gold at the end of the rainbow with that grin on his face. Sliding the door to the right, he spotted the green, bulging suitcase sitting in the far-left corner on the top shelf. He moved some blankets over to clear space to scoot the case over and put his hands on both sides of the avocado green rectangle to slide it from its assigned spot. Grabbing the handle once in sight, and not bothering to open it to see what awaited inside. Dad took it and locked it in his truck.

I was feeling not so hot about being a part of stabbing my own mother in the back, I decided to go to bed. Ella was still sitting at the dining table as if it were her divined perch earned from points garnered by turning on her friend. Oh, how I wished she would just stay at home in her big house so I never would see her, her tea leaves, or those weird cards ever again!

As I was in my little bed, I curled up tight, but no matter the position, sleep would not come, as knotted up as I felt inside. My heart again was pounding, and my head soon joined in with the band. I had not known the significance or probable consequences when I teased my mother about the letter dad had written to his girlfriend. How could I have known it would lead to the demise of our family? I paused a moment, "If I had known that dad was cheating on mom, would I have told mom? I was considered *her* girl as Selma was thought of as daddy's girl.

I was the one who loved her and would go with her places when Selma or dad did not. I admit though, I liked going places with her. Honestly, if I knew it was going to turn out like this, I might not have told her. As much of a scaredy cat as I was to talk to Bobby, I may have talked to him instead of her. It is possible we may not be here now. Here I am turning over to him her suitcase of feelings, thoughts, and secrets. I don't know what she had in her suitcase. I do know she guarded it and it was hers!

I did not like it when dad read my notes, found from my pockets at the dinner table. It was so embarrassing and mean-spirited, then he became my fortune teller of being beside the railroad with no shoes and pregnant and would end with a hearty laugh.

I am now complicit in the betrayal of my own mother! Beatings and all ugly behavior aside, this was an awful act. I do not hate my mother. I feared her. What if she finds out what I have done?

I yanked off my sheet and bedspread, my feet hit the floor, I ran toward the bathroom and vomited everything in me. Ella heard my retching. She opened the bathroom closet and took out a washcloth. Turning on the sink, she wet the cloth, wringing out the excess water, placed it on my forehead while holding my long hair back from my face. She said, "Now there little one, rinse your mouth and I will help you to bed."

Dad was standing in the hall as we edged out of the bathroom. Ella raised her hand and said to him, "I have her." She unrumpled my covers and let me slide back into bed. She placed the cool cloth on my forehead and wished me a restful night. Somehow that cool washcloth had the magic to take me away as I drifted off to sleep.

Ella returned day after day to sit at our aqua and white with chrome trim dining room table. She rarely ever got up from the matching and very padded vinyl chairs, with the exception to leave or to assist a vomiting girl. You would think she was sitting on a nest waiting for the eggs to hatch. There was no way to avoid her no matter if you came in the front or back door. There she was, sitting, trying to get you to speak to her. I preferred questions that only required a yes or a no answer and to slip away down the hall to our bedroom. Selma would just run past and wave. She and I even skipped getting a snack or kool-aid, to avoid the kitchen.

* * *

Smile Pretty While You Fall

The high school was in full swing with football games. The time-honored tradition of the Miss Garrett High School and class beauty pageant was soon announced. Each class 8th, 9th, 10th, 11th would nominate girls to participate. A ballot was made with all the nominations and passed to each homeroom to vote on their class choice. The top five nominees from the class vote would participate in the pageant. The process was the same for the 12th grade students. The winner was to be crowned, "Miss Garrett High School," at the culmination of the pageant.

I was stunned to be nominated and more so to be one of the top five to earn a spot on the court. However, I was at a disadvantage for I had never been in a pageant. I was a dancer, and it was considered an art form yet still it was not walking, turning, and doing all with a smile.

If my mother would have been present at home, I would have not been allowed to participate. It would not have been due to any adherence to a strict religious regulation. Nope, no daughter of hers would be allowed to parade around to be judged by her outward appearance only. Academic awards would have been allowed because it was earned, but no trophies for looking a certain way.

My friend's mom was nice to help with the dress which I brought home and planned to get ready there. My dad was going to take me. I was surprised and a little nervous. He sat with his arms across his body when he attended my dance recitals to demonstrate how thrilled he was to be attending. It was going to be in the high school gym which meant the Chief would be sitting on the wooden bleachers. I was not so sure how that was going to settle with him.

The evening arrived and I took a bath and washed my hair but after that I was clueless. I never wore makeup (which was okay because I did not have any). Nope, not even lipstick at age thirteen. My hair was styled as it always was, straight and long. I put my robe on over my slip because I did not want to take the chance to stain the dress in some way.

I walked down the hall into the kitchen where dad was standing with a dress shirt, a suit jacket and a pair of dress pants. I was surprised he had gone to that much trouble. He looked very handsome. He always looked *squared away*, his lingo. I guess I was expecting to see him in his navy uniform. He told me I looked pretty and asked me to sit down. He called Selma into the kitchen and had her take a seat. I was beginning to not like this table for I may not have tea leaves but could tell dad was going to spill something heavy.

I must be a gifted psychic because he did not disappoint. He went on to say he was going to take me to the high school and planned to bring me home. Dad went on to say, "Your mom has been in the hospital, and she is doing much better. She will be coming here, home tonight. She will be here when we get back. So, I will be dropping you off and then going back to the base."

I did not say anything at the weird looking doctor's office. I did not complain to dad when he came home the morning after the dragon was at the door. Nor did I tell Ella to mind her own business, every opportunity she tried to pry. I was not using the magic spigot trick I had learned to turn off the feelings and turn on the numbness. This time, I somehow found words to tell my dad, "It is not fair! I don't want her to come home. We are fine without her here. Dad don't let her come and ruin everything. Things were getting back to the way it used to be. Please, daddy don't let her come here."

He explained he could not stop her and not to worry about it right now before my big night. I stood in our dining room and cried, wondering how this could happen. I was no longer concerned about the school pageant, my dress, or anything else but my fast-beating heart. The pounding in my chest and then a sickening, sinking feeling of being defeated. Did it not matter that Selma and I had climbed out of windows and run around the neighborhood looking for sanctuary from our own screaming mother cussing us with every breath? The kids on the bus had finally stopped the chant, "Crazy Lady," when we boarded the bus. I guess that would start up again.

I pushed again, "Why does she have to come here, and come here tonight?! Why, can't you stay here with us like you have been, daddy?" Selma was in the hall watching and not saying a word. She was as quiet as we both were in the doctor's office at the hospital. Guess, she had never seen me act like I was, because I never had acted like that before.

Dad told me to go and get a cold washcloth to wash my face and get ready. It would soon be time for us to leave for the high school. Somehow, I could not shake this heavy sadness that sat down on me. It was like I was standing in plough mud and slowly sinking. It was so difficult to lift either one of my feet. My eyes were fixed on the hallway. My breathing was slowing its pace—I wished it would just stop all together. There was that cold, sharp pain running through me again becoming more dependable than the adults in my life.

Ella had arrived during my meltdown. She had stood frozen in place at the back door. She had somehow gotten a cold wet washcloth and was patting around my swollen eyes while she whispered softly, "Shhh now, everyting (Norwegian's just could not get the "th" sound), is going to be all right. You must stop crying. You are making your eyes puffy. Such a pretty girl." She reached down beside me and gathered my hands, handling them like they were delicate flowers, slightly pulling them. The rest of me slowly going down the hall toward the bedroom I shared with my sister. Ella was not the Disney she villain I had cast her to be, at least not at this moment.

Ella gently lifted my robe belt and loosened it, letting it fall to my side. Selma was in the room and quietly moving about, scooping up whatever Ella requested. Somehow, those two got my long, ivory colored dress with tiny, fuchsia-colored bouquets on over my head, zipped it up and bow tied it in the back. My sister brushed my hair without one word, no joke or smacking in my ear. She slipped my black heels on my feet, buckling the straps at my ankles. Meanwhile, Ella placed a pearl necklace on me, clasping it at the back of my neck. It was as if I was watching the two of them dress me and I was distanced from the whole scene playing out.

Ella sweetly kissed me on my cheek and said, "You are so pretty, Wanda. *Everyting* will be fine. You can tell us all about it soon. Now, go along. Your daddy is waiting." Somehow, I was able to make it down the hall to the front door and out to the truck where dad was waiting in the ranchero with the motor running. I opened the door and slid across the pick up's bench seat. This is one time it paid off that the Chief was so meticulous about the cleanliness of his vehicles. He looked at me and said, "You sure look pretty tonight, Wanda Lynn." I said a barely audible, "Thank you, daddy."

I do not know which one of us felt more awkward when we arrived and were standing in the high school gym, the Chief or me. Someone soon came along and told me to hurry up, all the contestants were to report on the stage behind the curtains. The awkwardness lingered as I looked to those rushing past me and then back at my dad. There he was in a dress shirt, a jacket, and a pair of dress pants. It was rare—like finding a gold brick alongside the road kind of rare—for Dad to be dressed up in civilian clothes. Yet, there Bob was, trying his best. He broke the silence by saying, "Now, you go on with your friends. I am going to find a seat," pointing to the bleachers. Oh my, the thought of the Master Chief Petty Officer of the US Navy sitting on the creaky, shaky wooden bleachers snapped my brain back from the fog where it had been lost without any breadcrumbs to lead it back until then.

Turning toward the stage, I lifted the front of my dress tiptoeing up the wooden steps beside the stage curtains. I was being ever so careful not to slip in my new shoes. I had practiced in them, as recommended by some of the girls that were more experienced., Being in even one pageant made everyone more experienced.

Pushing the heavy green velvet curtains aside enough to scoot by to access where the commotion was occurring. I relaxed a bit more when I spotted the girls in my grade standing together in a small circle. I was the last of the five selected eighth graders to arrive. There was my best friend smiling and saying hi as I stepped beside her. Another one of the girls told me she was glad I got there in time to have a picture. Adding, our group will be the first in line and they would soon call us as she pointed to the area with lights and a backdrop. A lady with a clipboard approached and asked my name. Checking my name on the list with her pencil, she asked what type of package I wanted. I must have looked confused because I was confused. She went on to quote prices and sizes of pictures. *I did not have any money. None of the papers I received at the pageant meetings had anything on it about photos or money.*

My friend, having seen that dazed look wash all over my face quite a bit lately, leaned over and said, "Go ask your dad for the money and I will hold your place." I nodded, then went back, slipping past the curtain, down the steps slowly and leaning against the wall as some of the upper-class girls (with their hair still in curlers, in flip flops, and carrying their dresses in garment bags in one hand above their heads, and their shoes in the other hand) walked past. Clearly, they knew what they were doing. I bet they had money for packages of photos.

I landed on the gym floor and looked for Bobby in the bleachers above where I left him. So many folks had come in since the few minutes we entered. There he was on the top row so he could rest his back against the wall. I was a bit surprised that he was there.

His arms were not crossed across his body, like I had seen at my dance recitals. I would call his look "Big Indian Chief" to my sister. It was not hard to see he was not happy to be in the audience for a dance recital no matter if he had a daughter in it or not.

I waved at him and winded my way through the assembled crowd that were chatting and searching for the best seat. Once, I reached him, he smiled and asked how it was going. I told him fine and went on about how many girls were behind the curtain. He looked at his watch, then my words tumbled out that he did not have to stay if he didn't want to, that he could come and pick me up later. He said he planned on staying and arranged where I was to meet him after it was over. Always prepared, my dad, --the Chief.

I returned to my group with my friend told me I was just in time to have my picture taken. The clipboard queen came over with an irritated face asking had I decided what package and I told her very quietly. She bent over and placed her ear closer to my face and I repeated that I could not have my picture taken because I did not have any money. Her face changed to a softer but more pitiful look nodding her head to acknowledge that she understood. The lady then told me they still wanted to take my photo saying it was needed for the yearbook. At least this will save me from explaining to the other girls why I did not have my picture taken. They did not know I had chickened out, not asking Bobby for the $8.00 to buy an 8x10, a 5x7, and 8 wallet sized photos.

The organized chaos continued as the groups of the upper-class girls were dressing, teasing hair, and having their photos snapped. Our group practiced our walk, acting as if we had a book on our heads so we would stand straight and not slump our shoulders. All the time at dance class helped me out with the walk and doing so in front of a crowd did not bother me.

We all admitted to one another of being nervous. One girl said she was going to throw up if we did not get started soon. Thank goodness she did not, and somehow, we all were lined up and ready to take the stage (in alphabetical order of course). Our group, being the youngest, was on the program to go first after the preliminary nods to sponsors. They gave the credit to those diligent ones who had worked so hard year after year to present the pageant for the high school. The emcee for the evening was announced and to whom much applause was given. Then finally, our group was instructed to go stand at the taped X on the stage.

I was the third one to take the stage. My head was up, shoulders back, smile in place and I walked into the stage lights on the wooden stage jetting out onto the gym floor. The emcee was a local television anchorman announcing our name, what school activities we were involved in and what occupation we planned on in the future. I had made about ten steps and my shoe stepped on the front hem of my dress pulling it down, causing me to misstep but luckily not fall. My confidence dipped and my smile had fallen only to return as a shaky toothy grin. All flushed, I made my turn and walked back down the stage to turn back around before I exited the stage. I knew if Bob was up there, he saw all of what happened. His head probably dropped as he shook his head then slowly leaned back against the wall while becoming The Big Chief, assuredly crossing his arms across his body.

Well, you guessed it, when our group lined up for the announcement of the winner over the school microphone—drum roll—it was *not* my name. Not shocked, yet I had a bit of hope. Yes, I was disappointed. I sure could have used a boost. The sting was soon covered with a shot of numbness.

My friend asked her mom if I could join them to have a late supper at a restaurant on the beach and then stay over. She went with me to ask Bob. I swear for a few moments I knew I could read his mind. I bet he thought, "Why did ya'll not make these plans sooner? I would not have had to sit through this entire girly girl thing on these wood boards with my back hurting." Ta-dah, a psychic is born! Dad agreed to let me go and he disappeared out of the crowded gym.

***

She Returns
and I Run

When I awoke the next morning, I knew I would have to go to the place that once was home. The dread of what I may find there was how I felt when friends were trying to convince me to go through the haunted house at the fair. At least the fair only came once a year, and I had a choice of opting to wait for them once they had the wits scared out of them. Going to the white brick house was not a choice.

Nausea had now become an immediate response when I knew I would have to talk to, or encounter, my mother. Leaving before anyone in my friend's house was awake was not uncommon these days for I had so little to say. Dressed in my pageant dress with my black heels. I took the time to tie the bow in the back so the ties would not be dragging behind me. Once I exited off the grass, laden heavy with dew, I dropped the hem of the dress I had bunched up in my hands to avoid getting it wet.

I made a click when I stepped on the road. It made me think of my tap shoes. These shoes were very similar to my tap shoes in shape and the ankle strap. I had not tightened my ankle straps, so the shoes were loose when I took a step. I could have tightened them up, making it easier to walk, but the slower pace just meant it would take a bit longer to walk to face *HER*.

This was probably the longest duration of time to walk such a short way. I even walked backwards at some point but stepped on the hem like I had the night before on stage, so I turned around. I grabbed some of the material in the front of the dress and hiked it up a couple inches to not be eating asphalt.

Arriving on Ventura Drive, I could see the black Gran Prix in the driveway. My heartbeat quickened and the want to run the other way was strong. My breath could not keep up with my heart rate, so I stopped in front of my neighbor's house. I was on the road, yet I had not seen any cars, or for that matter any dogs nor people stirring around. Taking slower breaths did not stop my fingers from tingling or the coating of protective numbness from setting in. I straightened my spine and went to the back door. Finding it unlocked, I reached down and pulled off my shoes.

I quietly stepped inside, pleading in my head for no one to be awake. Good, the house was quiet. I tip toed through the kitchen and dining room, reaching the hallway with wood floors and of course, there just had to be some spots that creaked. I moved down as quietly as I could in hopes of not waking anyone. I noticed the door to my mom's room was closed. What a relief, but I had a few more feet until I was to my room. I crossed a floorboard that made a high-pitched squeal, tattling on my presence. I stopped and held my breath, waiting for her door to fly open. Buzzing in my head started while I waited with my dress still pulled up to avoid tripping. I was frozen still in position, holding my shoes tightly in my left hand. When I needed to take a breath, I also took several fast steps placing me in my room. I reached behind me to shut and lock the door oh so quietly.

I noticed my sister was not in her bed and it was made so she had not slept there last night. The days of sleeping with our mom had long passed. Selma must have spent the night with a friend as well. She did not want to stay there any more than I did.

I untied the ties, unzipped the dress part way then yanked it over my head and dropped it on the floor inside out. Slipping on my gown and curling up in my own bed, I fell into a deep sleep.

Selma woke me up when she came in and flopped down on my bed. Thinking about where I was, my eyes snapped open looking toward our door and seeing that it and my mother's door were both open. My teeth gnashed together, I grabbed Selma's arm pulling her closer to me and said in a low voice, "Where is *she?*" Sis saw I was staring at the door, "Oh, Mom? She is in the kitchen. You want some French toast?"

"What? No, I don't want any French toast!" I replied with a disgusted tone as I pushed past her while climbing out of bed. I headed to the door, closing it quietly and making sure the lock was holding. Looking for some clothes to put on while gathering the dress from last night off the floor. I made my bed. Somehow, someway I was going to have to open the door and face what I feared down the hallway. I just did not want to.

Well, if things go bad, I can always take off out the door again. I decided to put on my canvas Keds just in case I had to run. My heartbeat knew I was headed toward trouble as it had started pounding against my chest wall *again*. If the good Lord assigned just so many heartbeats allowed per person, I was fast approaching my limit with as much pumping as mine had done in these past weeks.

The trip up the hall did not take half the time as the same distance traveled earlier toward my room. Then, there I was in the dining room with my mom placing French toast on a plate. She looked up to see me, turned to place the pan down and asked if I wanted something to eat, as she walked toward the table. She lay the plate at my place at the table. I shook my head no. Selma bounced in behind me telling Mom, "She does not want to eat."

Inga came around to the side of the table where I was standing. She pulled out a chair and slid down to sit. "I want to talk to you girls." She reached out and wrapped her hands around my wrists, pulling me toward her. I yanked my hands back to my side and stepped back a couple of steps bumping into Selma. She then pulled her chair out, sat down placing her elbows on the table and her hands under her chin balancing her head.

Surprisingly, Inga did not address my snap movements. She chose to start talking. "I know you both have been through a lot these past months with your dad moving out and I have not handled it well. I have had time to think about a lot of things." Her brown eyes were full of tears. "I am sorry for hurting you. I want you to know I love you both very much and promise things are going to be different from now on. I am asking you to give me a chance. Selma, will you give me a chance?" Selma said, "Sure", as she shrugged her shoulders. Then you guessed it, it was my turn. This time with her hands in her lap, Inga turned toward me and asked the same question. The tears were streaming down her face and her voice was shaky.

Oh, how I wanted to take off out the front door. No, I did not want to give her another chance but what choice did I have? It is not like we had anywhere else to live. Exhausted from all this turmoil, I nodded my head yes. My mother reached out and grabbed my waist and hugged me while she cried. I did not hug her back but did not pull away. I waited until she calmed herself so I could bolt from this scene. She tried to coax me to eat. I just could not. Instead, I asked for permission to go for a bike ride. No way was she going to tell me no after this family get together.

I could not get out of the house fast enough taking the path of least resistance going out the front door. The ceiling seemed to be lowering and the walls pushing in and soon I would have no air to breathe. Running to the back gate, pushing up the latch, I closed it quickly to avoid letting our little Pekingese, Bucky, out. He would run down a whole block before I could catch him and I wanted to be the one to run and not return. I grabbed the ugly three-speed green bike that Santa brought when Selma and I both had asked for ten speeds. No matter how uncool the bike was, it was the quickest way to get out of there. Sliding the bike past the gate without Bucky tagging along I pumped those pedals as hard as I could not sitting until I left our street far behind. Now, where was I to go? I headed to the boat landing to stare at the Ashley River hoping an answer would jump up like the fish did sometimes.

Crazy Lady with a K-nife

Selma seemed ok with the situation of mom being home, but she scooted over to the race car shop every weekend. Dad had been coming to pick her up. One afternoon when he stopped over, he had went to the large garage in the backyard for a tool or something. It is possible Inga had seen him go out there and waited for him to come back. He opened the back gate and started his way out.

I was standing out at the street to just say hi. I then saw Mom appear. I yelled at Dad to move. He turned and saw her with a knife. He squatted as she thrusted downward with knife in her hand. He grabbed her forearm demanding her to drop it. After a few shakes, she dropped it. She was shrieking and crying like a wild, wounded mountain cat. Dad had cleared the fence, locking her on the other side and scooted into his truck. Selma jumped in and they left.

Mom continued her wailing as neighbors came out of their houses to see what was making that noise. I knew and was not going to stop to hear her version. It had played out before me. The crying started *again*! I was so angry and so embarrassed, yet another scene created by my mother. Screeching like a jungle bird from some unknown exotic land, "Your father took my suitcase to his lawyer. They are going to use it on court. How did he know about my suitcase?" She reached out and called my name, pleading me to come help her. "You know when I was in the hospital? I had tried to end my life by taking a bunch of sleeping pills. You know what *your father* said to me? Do you? He said, I could not do anything right. I could not even kill myself!" She was sobbing, as she bent over at the waist coughing and spitting on the sidewalk.

Frozen in place as if my feet were melded to the pavement, I listened and watched her put on a show for all to see and hear. I shook myself loose. I had to run, but not toward her. No, I quickly turned and ran down Ventura to Paramount in flip flops, as fast as I could run. I was scared and sickened by what I had just viewed. My mother could have killed my father. At least, that looked like her intent from my view—being directly in front of them with no obstructions. The words she spewed for everyone's consumption. He wanted her to die. What was I to do? I could not digest the things spoken.

I ran up a block to Darlene Street and there was a group of neighborhood friends talking on the corner—one was a boy my age who I knew well, Ronnie. We hung out together in the neighborhood, school, and sometimes at the racetrack. He was standing still, keeping his bike balanced between his legs and bouncing the handlebars between his hands. He held his arms wide open as I approached the group.

I slowed and he grabbed me saying, "What's wrong?" No one had asked all these weeks if anything was wrong, but Ronnie asked. He did not let go of my arms. I stopped in place. I had come to detest the sound of my mother's crying. I tried not to do the same. I leaned my head in close to him and when he patted my back, I wept as quietly as one could when your life seems shattered.

Kids from my road had run after me then started to walk as they approached the huddle. One of the boys whispered, "What happened?" Tommy, my next-door neighbor quietly answered, "Her mom lost her mind again."

Ronnie nodded his head, signaling he understood why his friend was sobbing in his arms. This is something thirteen-year-old boys are not used to doing. Somehow, at his young age, he did the kindest act with such ease. I calmed soon and pulled away slowly, telling him thank you. He asked what I was going to do. This was different from the night runs, which he had served as bike patrol to keep Sis and I informed on the black Gran Prix's prowl. This was in the middle of the day and if she decided to drive around looking for me, it was much harder to hide. I told him the friend's house I was headed toward. He told me to go on and they all would watch out until I got there. I knew the whistles of those on the bike patrol. He rode his bike with others tagging along down Paramount turning on Ventura. I looked as he nodded, letting me know I was clear. Some of the other riders rode to the next road (Mimosa) and came up the other way on Ventura.

I returned home on Sunday afternoon. Selma had been dropped off by someone other than my dad for obvious reasons.

Deny and Pretend

Another school week started and each day we came home to a note on the table along with a snack. My mother was working as a waitress downtown. She would come home soon after we arrived. If our homework and chores were completed, we could go out to see our friends if we were back by supper time.

School was my haven. It was a place where I flourished. I could be the girl I was before life at home imploded. My grades were in good standing. I had been elected to Student Council.

I enjoyed going to football and basketball games with my friends. The games were well supported with the stands full of students, parents and alumni cheering on the Falcons to victory. The cheerleaders were the best around. They were really into the game (be it football or basketball). They led cheers appropriate to the plays on the fields, points on the board or timing of the game. The cheerleaders were often hoarse by the third quarter or third period—athletic and acrobatic—leading the crowds to boost our team on for the win. The crowds responded to them calling out school initials and responding to the other school's challenge of "We Got More" (meaning more spirit).

Attending a Garrett High School game was not just going to a game, it was an event. The crowd would start bits of songs and stomp their feet in rhythm on the aluminum bleachers. (Keep in mind these were the days of Kool and the Gang, Queen and KC and the Sunshine Band.) I'll never forget singing to the opposing team at the end of the game if we reigned as the victors, "*We shall not be, We shall not be moved, Just like a tree standing in the water, We shall not be moved.*" And kicking in, "*Na Na Na, Hey, Hey Goodbye.*" The pep band came in at times setting the mood right, to pump up the feeling when they played a great rendition of, "The Horse."

At school we bought spirit ribbons to be worn days leading up to a game. I had placed mine on the dresser mirror at home. I was gaining quite a nice collection of red, white, and blue ribbons. My favorite were the white spirit ribbons with a gold football/basketball at the top that had adhesive on the back of the ball to stick on the ribbon to keep it in place on your clothes.

There were all kinds of clubs to belong to for students with different interests; water skiing, photography, and bike clubs (to name a few). Those clubs often would have dances as fundraisers to be held in the cafeteria or gym.

What a great place! Many students were military brats although I did not know that fact until much later in life. We were a diverse lot and it seemed to work well.

Garrett High had two separate lunch periods. My schedule was the first lunch. I had never eaten school lunch. I always took my lunch from home in elementary school. I did not eat breakfast as a teenager so I became hungry about eleven a.m. Lunch time was not too long after my tummy would start growling. I often had a pack of crackers. There was always one of the clubs or athletic groups having some sort of fundraiser selling M&M's or some other candy. It squashed the hunger until I arrived home to raid the pantry for cereal.

Most of my friends were scheduled for second lunch opening the opportunity to make new friends. That was usually not an issue being a navy brat due to attending many different schools. You learn kids usually ask your name and where you were from, or you were the one to ask. You develop the skills needed to meet people when your world had influx of new people on a regular basis. People were like pool toys, always bopping around. Some floated over to the side. Some may swim after you and if it was one of your favorites, you may swim after them.

If they were picked up, moved away, and gone, you would miss them. You may think about them, perhaps talk to someone who shared a class or swimming lessons with them. Once they were out of the pool, you started to talk to others bopping around in the same area you were bopping around. If you had some things in common and they were nice, you kept swimming around together. If not, then you both usually went bopping in another part of the pool.

The high school was a much bigger pool. It would be a bit different because, for the first time, students mixed it up with students from other grades. Students from the upper classes had the same lunch time as I did. There was no assigned seating where your class sat at the same table along with your teacher.

There was a new-found freedom. You were welcome to go to the cafeteria or not. It was within guidelines to be outside on the school campus. Not being a fan of the smell of the cafeteria, I would stay outside. I waited on the stoop of an annex building because my next class was scheduled on the first floor. It was the only class on my schedule that was not an honors class. The subject was earth science. I knew it would be difficult for me to hang with it because, well I found it to be quite boring.

It was this teacher, Mrs. Gadsen who would be the toughest teacher I would encounter that year. She had order in her classroom. She would not tolerate joking and stopped unwarranted comments by raising her head and just looking up at the students. I never pushed my luck, making sure I was in her class and seated by the time the second bell rang.

I did, however, wait to enter the building. I had noticed a boy scheduled with the same lunch time. I waited until he had passed by before entering the building. I was hoping he would notice me and stop by to talk. I did learn his name from another student. He was in a grade ahead of me. I was careful to only ask one person, so it did not fly from person to person that I was interested before I was sure if I was or not. The boys in my grade were still running up and down the halls throwing paper and shouting at one another. Somehow, the older boys not participating in such raucous behavior, seemed more suited to being in high school.

This very, specific boy had dark brown hair and blue eyes. He wore Levi corduroys with the red tag sewn into inside of the right back pocket seam. He did not run to class or throw paper at other boys. No, he just walked confidently, head held up, a nice stride, and he complimented the Levi pockets so very well.

After a week or two, I grew weary of waiting to see if he would stop to talk to me. He had begun to slightly smile—The kind of smile you cannot help from sliding across your face even when you are trying your dead level best for it not to slip out. Yeah—that kind of a smile. I was not sure if it was, "Hey, I see you and I am interested," or "Hey there, little girl, it is cute that you are sitting there to watch me walk by. Now, go away," kind of smile.

I had a change of plans. I would walk a different route during lunch and not hang so close to the door, maybe loiter over close to the other building. (Hey, I still wanted to make it to class on time.) I was walking on the sidewalk in front of the school, readying to take the turn to the side of the school in between it and the football field. I noticed a few feet ahead of me was Levi guy stepping up onto the sidewalk. I do not know what possessed my mouth to open but he looked up to see me walking toward him and **I** said, "Hello. You got a minute? I would like to talk to you," Yes, I did! I had not rehearsed this in my mind, so I was flying solo without any practice. I had *never* been this bold, ever, about anything or anyone.

He responded as he slipped his hands in his front two pockets, "Yeah, sure." I told him my name and asked him for his name. I already knew but did not want him to know I knew his name (Wayne). I added, "Do you have a girlfriend, Wayne?" He smiled that slight smile and said, "I did but we broke up." He told me her name and guess what? I knew her. She lived one street up from my house and she and I had shared a "like" of another boy before. "Great, here we go again," I thought—thankfully I did not say it out loud for Levi guy to hear.

Being bold as I could be, I just jumped right out and mentioned I had noticed we shared the same lunch. He nodded and I made direct eye contact with those blue eyes. Mercy, I was starting to lose whatever had overtaken me and pushed me to continue to embarrass myself. I voiced—out loud—that I thought he was cute, and I would like to be his new girlfriend. No, wishy washy talk. I dove straight in for all or nothing. If you are wondering if my heart was pounding—it was like someone was trying to knock down a brick wall inside my chest. I was a little dizzy. It was a good thing I did not eat lunch because I would have lost it right there on the sidewalk. I am sure that would have left an everlasting impression, not the one I would have liked either.

He reached out and took my hand. He had really, nice hands. His nails were clean, and I liked the shape of his fingers. My tiny hand was engulfed by his much larger hand. I had not ever felt this glowing kind of wonderful. As bold as I was, you would think I would have not been near as breathless and quiet. We walked together toward the annex building for our time was up due to the first bell had just rung. Honestly, I do not think I heard it at all. Mr. Blue Eyes said he would meet me after class as he headed for the stairs to take him to his class on the second floor. Stunned, yet somehow, I floated to my science class a couple doors down the hall on the right.

One of my new science class friends, Greg, whispered, "I just saw you holding hands with a ninth grader." I just nodded my head up and down as I slid down the back of my seat and landed with my bottom on the wooden platform of the chair. After the last few months, I had learned to turn my feelings on and off to protect me from overstimulation of the hurt that had been heaved on by the shovel full. This felt like that protective coating of numbness, yet I had not flipped the switch. It had to be a shock. Maybe it has been shocking all the other times and I had not learned any magical trick to keep myself from being broken in body, mind or spirit.

My head was spinning with all types of thoughts. Second guessing if what just happened really happened. Maybe, Levi guy was making fun of me and when class is over and he meets with me, he will have his friends with him and he will make fun of me for thinking he would be my boyfriend, by pointing and laughing at me. Oh no, what have I done? Is it possible he knew that the kids on my bus said, "Crazy Lady" when my sister and I got on the bus? What a stupid, impetuous thing I have done!

Mrs. Gadsen asked me why I had not opened my book. I shook my head as she opened my book to the page we were on and pointed where the class, except for me, was currently focused. My mind never got into the groove on the lesson that day. I may have stared at the page and turned the page cued by my classmates, yet my brain was frozen on the gesture of an outstretched hand by Levi guy. The class session seemed suspended in time. I was not staring at the clock. It was like we all were just stuck there and no plans to dismiss.

The bell rang and I was usually one of the first rushing out the door to make it to upstairs in the main building for algebra class, not this time. I was in slow motion, gathering my book and papers like lead was weighing each movement. I was not sure if he would be there or not. I had to know, therefore I sped it up rushing up to the door. Slowing it down as I walked out the door trying not to appear as if I was searching for anyone. I looked up from the mess I had made with my books and papers to see those blue eyes connect with mine. We exchanged phone numbers and he said he would call me that night.

He did as he said and called. The phone rang and I lunged for the phone like a long jumper in the Olympics. Attempting to be calm however, I was nearly out of breath when I answered the phone. He asked for me by name. It was nice to hear him say my name. His voice was measured with a nice tone being male, but not a little boy's voice. Certainly, it was nice to hear on the other end of the phone.

The next few weeks were spent seeing one another at school and talking on the phone at night. He had advanced to playing songs on his guitar and singing along with songs on the radio. We talked of school and what we wanted in the future, our futures. He was the one making it a "shared" future by talking about places we would live. It was a stark distance from what was happening in my home life as our family slipped further into an empty vacuum.

I was spending every possible moment at school, attending any games, events or dances offered. Wayne had asked me to meet him at the next dance. I happily agreed although we did not dance together very much, only a slow song or two. He may have been too nervous to ask. I was too ridden with anxiety to dance with the girls, leaving him to view me. Although, I could really dance, especially on a stage with a routine, or at home with the records playing on the stereo. When we had race car parties I would dance all night long, not minding who was watching. This was different though.

The dance concluded and students were filing out. My mother was to pick me up. Wayne lived nearby the school and planned to walk home. He stood with me out in front of our school as I waited for my mom. Everyone left, teachers had locked up and checked with us. I told them my mom was coming to get me.

It had been thirty to forty-five minutes after the dance and still no one had shown to pick me up. Although I tried to play it off, my nerves were all out of whack. Then I saw Michael riding his bike on the road in front of the school. His mother and mine were friends and known to go out together on too many occasions. He lived with his dad. His sisters lived with his mother, two streets above the rented white brick house where my family resided. I yelled out and asked him to see if his mother could tell my mom to come and pick me up. Michael said,

"Yeah." I felt somewhat better. I knew he would do what he could to get the message to his mom.

There was a third person there hanging with Wayne. I told them both they could leave that it should not be too long before someone came and picked me up. Honestly, I would have walked home had Wayne not been there despite having to cross a four-lane highway at night. Actually, I would have run home because I would have been too freaked out standing outside in the dark.

Wayne refused to leave me standing there, thank goodness. It was approximately twenty minutes after waving Michael down when headlights appeared turning to the front road of the school. It was not the black Gran Prix that I had run away from many times. It was a smaller car and made noises a car makes when it is attracting the attention of a mechanic.

Wayne, recognizing our time was soon to be over leaned over and gently kissed me. It was not the first time I had noticed his full, thick lips but it was the first time I had felt them on my mouth. It almost made me forget where I was but the noise from the car brought me back to my predicament.

It was Michael's mother and his sister, Rosie (who was a year older than me). She and I were friends. It was really nice seeing her face after being stood up by my own mother. Mrs. Rogers told me to get in the car and she would take me home. Wayne told me good night and we could talk later.

I got in the back seat as Mrs. Rogers drove me home. She pulled up in the driveway of what had been known as home. The garage door was up with the garage light on. It provided a visual of my mother on the back steps to the kitchen door with a man I had not seen or met. Mrs. Rogers stepped out of the car holding the back seat up so I could get out. Her daughter stepped out of the other side. I walked toward the garage so slowly, almost as if I was being pushed toward the scene in front of me. Eventually, I called out for my mother. She raised her head, turning to look out of the garage. I mentioned she had not come to pick me up from the dance. She spewed out a few slurred words indicating she had been drinking as her physical movements also demonstrated. Asking who the man was only produced an inaudible blurb. Mrs. Rogers said, "Inga, your daughter is home so whoever this is, needs to leave." Inga then verbally exploded, "This is where I live. Let her go somewhere else. He is not going anywhere!" Expletives were screamed as Mrs. Rogers instructed me to get back in the car. Gently touching my shoulders and turning me in the direction of her car, she guided my body back to the driver's side and lifted the back seat so I could slide into the back seat again. She reassured me that I could stay at her house. Inga continued to scream and was spitting as we rolled out of the drive.

Once again, I was too exhausted and numb to be embarrassed. Mrs. Rogers was very caring, attempting to smooth things over saying something like my mom was drinking and not thinking. She added that she loved me and would not have done that if she had not been drinking. The words caused it to hurt like a deep knife wound below the heart was yanked downward toward the belly and hot blood was oozing and pooling on the inside. The ice-cold returned to squelch the fire and save the host as I thought of the mad, rabid foam, frothing from Inga's mouth making her barely able to speak let alone stand on the steps of the house we once lived in as a family.

Despite the sights I had seen, my sleep came fast and hard. Once again, thanks for all the grace of friends. Leaving a friend's house before they awoke so there would not be this awkward feeling of, "What do we do with her now?" It was not like I was a stray cat that you could let out and tell it to shush and go home. I had slept in my clothes, always a great feeling to wake up all crumpled and material bunched up in places you wish it were not. I left a note on the kitchen table saying thank you for all the help. I apologized that they had to come out late to come get me. I did not write it down but sure thought I was sorrier for what they viewed when they took me home. I signed my name and then tried to quietly open the door. What is it about doors that you attempt to slip out of without disturbing anyone that make so many cracking and squeaky sounds? I should have been equipped with a run-away kit stocked with WD-40, crackers, flip flops, band-aids, and a blanket.

Finally, on the porch with the loud door securely closed, I slid my shoes on over one foot with a sock and the other without a sock. I was doing the walk of shame before I ever heard the saying. I did know how the shame felt although it may have been for different reasons. It still felt sickening. It was even more sickening if you did not know what you would find once you arrived at your lovely home.

I always turned down Ventura Drive looking for the black Gran Prix. It was not parked cockeyed in the drive like it had been last night. The car may be in the garage and if it is—with as little wiggle room to maneuver when not drinking—it is going to be banged up down both sides. I followed my usual pattern by checking through the back door of the garage before I knew whether it would be safe to go in or not. I was not sure where that car was, yet I was thrilled as I could be that it was not in the garage. It was a clear sign I could go on in.

As I entered the back door, noticing there was glass broken on the steps that looked like from some type of bottle. I was not going to sweep this mess up (at least not right now). The kitchen had dirty dishes piled up in the sink and the table had used utensils on the placemats along with glass rings on the corners. The tablecloth was askew, yet I walked right on by. It was not my mess, not mine to clean up. I peaked in what had been my parent's bedroom and dang if it was not another squealing door. Luckily, there was no one in there to bother although the sheets and pillows were tossed all about. I was not even going to think about it.

I went to my room and took a clean nightgown from the bottom drawer. I went off to take a bath to feel better about myself. I'm not sure why a bath helps you sift through some things, maybe it is the water washing away worries. Whatever it is, it is the closest thing to magic I have for treating this whole mess. I leaned back to stretch out to wet my hair to give it a good shampooing. The aroma therapy for the smell of the shampoo had lifted this girl's spirits. I had soon scrubbed all I possibly could then exited the tub. I always remembered to clean it when I had completed my bath. Even if the rest of the house was in disarray, I was not adding to it. I gently patted myself dry. My hair was wrapped in the towel, so I scrubbed with the towel as if I was shampooing my hair all over again. I placed my night gown over my head and down over my waist. I was not too sure if I may be putting on a show once I opened the bathroom door these days. Looking up and down the hall and seeing not a soul in sight I glided to my room, shut, locked the door, and pushed my sister's bed against the door. Everything was so unpredictable. It was just smart planning to have a little notice if I needed to be heading out the window like a bird when its birdcage door had been left open.

A tap on my bedroom door along with an insistent, "Come on. Open up the door, Wanda," said my sister. I pulled myself out of my bed to push the blockade away to get to the lock on the door. Selma was patient for a change. She knew the why for the blockade. I opened the door, headed back to my bed when she said, "Come on with me. Dad brought me home and he wants to talk to us." I replied in a cranky but low tone, "Again?" "Yes, again. Now come on."

There he was sitting in his recliner. It was not in the lay on back position. This was going to be an all too familiar serious talk. I knew neither one of us were in trouble. How could we be? We were too busy running away from it.

Dad started by saying the police called him the night before about a disturbance at the house. He asked if I knew anything about it. I told him all that I knew, beginning with waiting for mom to come pick me up to leaving with Mrs. Roger. Dad listened carefully. When I concluded with my information, he asked if I knew where mom was. I told him the car was gone when I came home earlier. He sat there looking at Selma and me, then at the floor. He said he had talked to the family that Selma has been staying with some of the time and they are willing to let her stay there for a little while as he got things straightened out. Turning to me, he asked if there was anyone that would allow me to stay with them. I mentioned two families. The one family I had been attending church with, and I frequently spent the night on the weekend. They had five children. I did not want to ask them because they would say "yes" but I felt it would put them out too much. Dad reminded me; he was going to be the one to ask.

My best friend and I started to not be as close as before mostly because at high school we did not have classes together. We both were meeting new people and doing different activities. I told Dad I would like to stay with her if it was possible.

He asked that I get a few things together and we would take a ride over there to talk to her parents. I changed my clothes, stuffed a few clothes in a grocery bag along with my toothbrush, toothpaste, and a few other items. Feeling rushed, I quickly headed out to Dad's truck, crammed my bag in the floorboard and scooted beside my sister. We rode over to a block and half away pulling up to my friend's house. I directed Dad to the back door, explaining no one ever went to the front door. It seemed to make him uncomfortable to be so casual.

***

Lost in the Woods

I knocked on the door of my best friend's house. She opened the door eating a piece of toast. When she saw it was my dad with me, she dropped her hand with the toast and hid it behind her back. She looked over to her parents sitting at the kitchen table. Her dad stood up and walked over to Bobby, extending his hand. My friend looked at me widening her eyes as if to say, "Hey, what's up?" Well, we were standing right there so I could not tell her. I barely shrugged my shoulders so the grown-ups could not read anything into our attempt of sign language.

The dads shook hands. My dad asked if he could speak to him and the mom in private. Good, we were released to go talk and that allowed me to catch Caroline up on the reason for the meeting of the chiefs. She had known about the ongoing saga of chaos on the Ventura block. If I had talked about it all, it was with her. It was her mother that had gotten my dress for the pageant. They may have known more than I did about the who and whys of it all.

Caroline rushed me down the hall to her room and I told her about the recent upheaval. I added that Dad had been contacted so he is required to act. The navy housing would not permit The Chief, to bring his two daughters to reside with him and the other chiefs. My sister was in the truck waiting to be deposited over at the Wells'. She was pretty much living there most of the time anyway.

I told Caroline that Dad was in their kitchen pitching a plea for me to stay with her until he could make other arrangements. My thoughts had not wandered down that lane yet. When you are in fight or flight mode (mine being flight most of my waking moments) the brain was otherwise occupied. This time was not the time to start thinking about what the plans entailed. I had found going from moment to moment was the only way to function.

The only plan I was concerned about were the ones being discussed in Caroline's kitchen. I coaxed her to sneak down to check if we could hear anything. Of course, by the time we got to a decent eavesdropping point, the conversation was wrapping up. Caroline's dad called out for her. We popped right in not being too obvious due to the heavy level discussion.

I went and stood beside my dad. He explained that the Gaines' had agreed to allow me to stay with them for a short while. He reminded me to be well behaved and listen to them. He added if I needed anything to let Caroline's mom or dad know and they would get in touch with him.

All I could do was shake my head. For some unknown reason to me, I wanted to cry. A lump had developed in my throat as I was holding back the tears. Dad went on instructing me that, Mrs. Gaines had my lunch money so I should be set for school in the morning.

The tears puddled up when Dad mentioned school in the morning. I gasped. He asked, "What?" I was scared but I uttered out, "My book bag with homework was at home." Dad replied, "It's no wonder, the way we rushed out of the house." I looked up at him with a face too easily read if he was not distracted. My face was saying, "Who is this man with great understanding and empathy and why does he look so much like my father?" Somehow it was decided, or perhaps Caroline volunteered to go to the house to get my bookbag. Dad gave her the key.

The Gaines' and Dad made small talk sitting around the table while awaiting the return of Caroline. I was talking with her older sister, Olivia. I loved hanging out with her much more than Caroline. We did many quiet things together; played board games, puzzles, and paint by number for hours. I felt accepted by her. I was never in a place of competition with Olivia.

***

Caroline was another subject. Although, I had claimed her as my best friend, my feelings had changed somewhat. Months prior, I had come over to say goodbye before their family vacation to Las Vegas. (*The next night was when I had taken off from my Mom and ended up sleeping in the Gaines' garage on the washer and dryer.*) She had hesitated taking me to her room, which was odd. We always went into her room.

Once we entered, it was plain for me to see in brightly, colored lights on her Lite Brite screen. "Caroline loves Michael." The pegs said it all, my best friend liked my boyfriend! She told me she was sorry and added a kick to the gut by saying he liked her too. I just left her room without another word. I left the door open, walked down the hallway along the thick plastic carpet protector over the white carpet. Caroline did not follow or call out my name. I crossed over to the living room (or maybe it is the family room because the house did have a formal living room that no one ever went in). The family room did not have carpet. It was more like a brick linoleum.

I could see Caroline's father through the sliding glass doors, working out in the yard in his white t-shirt. It was not an unusual sight. He was always outside working on some project. An impressive project was a recovered brick barbeque grill on the patio.

The kitchen door seemed like a football length away due to me feeling like I was stuck on a conveyor belt, moving ever so slowly. Once the kitchen was reached, I slipped on my shoes at the back door. I grabbed the kitchen doorknob then I took a deep breath as I opened the door. I must not have taken a breath since leaving the room. It was like when you fall off the monkey bars, landing on the ground looking up, and your back hurts straight through to your chest. That hurts so much that you dare not take a breath for certain that the pain is going to intensify. Eventually, you must take a breath because *if you are not breathing nothing else matters.*

The breathing became easier as I quietly walked to Ventura Drive. The energy to run or cry was not there. Good thing I knew this route, for my head was foggy. My insides felt shaky, empty, unsure of anything real. I tried to block thinking of what just happened because each time I replayed the scene in Caroline's room it left me with the impression that my feelings did not matter to her in the very least. She was matter of fact and did not flinch telling me the few words she spoke. I trusted her and felt like her sister. In comparison, the treatment was similar to what my sister would have done when it comes to dealing with boys. No matter, I still was stunned.

The Gaines' left for their family vacation early the next morning as did my illusions of friendship.

* * *

Caroline returned with my bookbag very quickly. I heard when she came in the back door. Her mother sounded louder and higher pitched than what I am accustomed to hearing from her soft toned voice. Olivia and I looked at each other and knew something were not quite right, so up we went to the kitchen. There stood Caroline with the chiefs and her mom standing around her. Her curly blonde hair that is always with every hair in place was all messed up on top of her head. Her face was flushed from its porcelain color, and it appeared there were scratches on her right-side cheek and her neck. Caroline always wore nice clothes and the ones she had on were nice, but it was obvious the sweater's neck was stretched out.

The adults were so busy asking questions she did not have time to hear them much less answer any of them. Her mom began to smooth her hair and attempt to rearrange her sweater which was pulled out of shape. She pulled her daughter closer to her and the questions stopped. Caroline placed my bookbag down beside her on the floor. "Caroline, tell me what happened." Caroline raised her head up and took a deep breath. She explained when she arrived at the house, she knew to look for the car because I did that and even though the car was not there, she rang the doorbell. No one came to the door, and it was quiet. Caroline placed the key in the lock of the front door and called out to see if anyone was home. When no one answered, she entered the house and went to my room to pick up the book bag.

She started down the hall then looked up to see Inga standing in front of her. Caroline said she tried to step by her, but Inga grabbed her by her hair. Her fingers wrapped in Caroline's hair, she yanked her toward the living room. Caroline went on to explain she had held onto her own hair and managed to pull her hair away from my mother, leaving some of her hair laced in my mother's fingers. Bolting her way to the door, Inga scratched her face and neck attempting to detain her further. Caroline pushed Inga away with both hands. Inga was incensed.

How dare she?! She lunged toward Caroline, managing to get a hold of the collar of her sweater, but Caroline kept pulling away, finally freeing herself from the drunken woman. Inga fell on the floor exhausted from wrestling with the young woman. She resorted to just yelling slurred obscenities, allowing Caroline the time to make it to the door and run. She ran all the way home with the book-bag in hand.

A deafening, flat silence consumed the room despite having so many people with more to say without knowing when to form the words. Mrs. Gaines, being a mother, initiated the first move, telling Caroline to come with her to the bathroom to wash up. Caroline nodded, moving forward from the huddled crowd. Leaving the chiefs face-to-face. My daddy followed up with, "I apologize for my wife's in-excusable behavior. I understand if you change your mind about the agreement." Mr. Gaines huffed and put his hand to his forehead raking through his thick, black, wavy hair. He took in another breath, invited Dad to have a seat and give him a moment to talk to his wife. Dad sat back down at the kitchen table looking at his watch. This is the first since our visit that I saw the dad that I knew. The impa-tient—get it done and move on to the next task— Dad.

Olivia noticed my tension. She left my side to pick up the coffee pot and offer some to my dad who was becoming more like Sitting Bull. Surprisingly, he pleas-antly accepted. I was leaning against the door frame between the family room and the kitchen as if I were part of the opening itself. What do you say when your monster mother attacks a friend that is considered a child? Somehow, I am sorry is not quite appropriate. I was waiting to know if I could be a guest in their home.

Yes, glued to the frame between the rooms I could hear the discussion of the Gaines' standing in the hallway despite their attempts to whisper. Mrs. Gaines quite understandably was opposed to me remaining a guest in their home for fear that the acts of my mother may heighten. She added they may need to call the police for the beating of Caroline that had just occurred. Mr. Gaines disagreed with calling the police mentioning that Chief Lefler has had more than his share of trouble in dealing with his wife including explaining it to the navy. He felt there would be no harm. After all, he reminded Mrs. Gaines, he was always at the house after work.

Besides, he pointed out, that if things became out of hand, then they could call Chief Lefler to come to pick up the girl. Caroline sounded in with her want-ing me to stay, complete with—she felt sorry for me. Mrs. Gaines gave in to her daughter's good Samaritan pleas agreeing the girl can stay for a short time but if there is a moment of trouble Chief Lefler will be called to come and get her.

Chief Gaines returned to the kitchen and sat down across from Chief Lefler. No wonder world peace is never achieved with all the negotiations necessary with details, various points to consider, then negotiation again.

All discussions completed; dad headed out to the truck where my sister had been uncharacteristically patient. I walked out with him and then realized why she was not banging on the door. Some of the neighborhood friends were standing around talking with her. As soon as dad appeared she hopped in the truck, ready to go. Dad gave me a side hug and reminded me again to behave. He probably did not know what else to say. It was not like I was a delinquent or even close to being one.

I waved bye and wanted to run after them but knew there was no reason. It would only prolong matters. I turned, swallowed my tears, and went inside a place I was not truly wanted, not much different from home. Thank heavens for Olivia.

Staying at the Gaines' was not a bad place to land for a little while. No one brought up my mother at all, not even the altercation between Caroline and her. I was ever so grateful. I was required to do chores at home and had helped there at the Gaines' many times including the wiping dust off artificial plants. I did not see the reason to have plants that were not real that you had to dust, but I was not in position to debate so I dusted leaf by leaf.

My phone time with Wayne was non-existent. Although, I let him know I was not staying at home. I did not tell him what all was happening. We saw each other at school and if there were after school activities. Lunch time was a big deal to me because I was spending time with someone that liked me with no judgements attached. Of course, he did not know, or at least if he did, he did not say anything.

***

My attention for everything that required sitting down, to focus or study was replaced with distracting thoughts of: *What is my dad planning? Where are we going to live? Who are we going to live with?* Coming up with the correct answer for a math equation, composing a poem for English class or trying to distinguish the different types of rock—sedimentary or igneous—in science class was overwhelming. My grades dropped but I thought I was the only one to notice until one day after science class, Mrs. Gadsen asked me to stay after class. She came to the front of her desk. Standing, she started to talk about noticing I had been different lately. She noted my grades were not showing my ability. She inquired as to what was going on with me, causing me to behave this way.

I sat there with my head dropped, looking at the desk. Mrs. Gadsen was insistent for an answer. She had a reputation for being tough. Now, the questions were not asked in a syrupy, sweet as expected from another teacher. No, her inquiries were direct and bold, cutting through any small talk.

The sad thing is no one else had noticed. No one cared enough to look and say "Wait a minute, something is going on here." Mrs. Gadsen, asked, and I could not answer her. I burst into tears, sobbing out loud, not able to form words. It was what is called an ugly cry. Mrs. Gadsen did not expect such a response. She grabbed a tissue box and came forward, softening her voice. I told her I was not staying at home, and neither was my sister due to my parent's divorce proceedings. I did not know what was going to happen to me or my sister. I added that my mother had been in the hospital, and I did not know what to do.

Mrs. Gadsen was moving about, obviously uncomfortable with this student pouring her heart out. She did not know what to do either. She paced a bit and then came up with a plan to send me to the guidance counselor. The guidance office was a door down from her classroom. Mrs. Gadsen handed me some more tissues, helped me gather my books, and escorted me next door straight to the counselor's office door. I guess she was not expecting her talk to open a Pandora's box and was probably relieved to return to her classroom alone.

The counselor and I had a brief session. She suggested a meeting with one of my parents. I was less than thrilled. So much for someone listening or trying to help fix this mess. I wondered if my sister had these uncomfortable, yucky feelings of doom as if our world was collapsing while everyone else stood around. They saw us falling through a crack in the earth's surface yet all they did was look and kept on watching. It is not like Selma, and I had any time to talk about it. I was having a hard enough time getting through the day to much bother to talk to anyone. What was there to say, anyway?

A few days went by when I was called to the counselor's office. When I arrived there in the office seated in one of the chairs was my mother. The anger I felt to be in the same room with her was like a wildfire. I wanted to explode, to become a fire breathing dragon opening my mouth to let loose flames. I asked the counselor, "Why is *she* here?" She explained, "Remember, when we spoke, I told you that I was going to need to have one of your parents when we met next. Well, I could not get a hold of your dad, but your mom agreed to come."

For several minutes the counselor was asking questions to understand the background of the situation. My mother was answering them all in a soft victim type voice pausing to cry every little bit. I was sitting in the other chair in a very cramped office, arms crossed over my stomach, mouth clenched, rolling my eyes. The question from the counselor requesting my response was, "Where would you like to live?" I replied quickly, "In a tent on the football field. I wish I never had to leave school." The counselor clarified her inquiry, "Which parent would you prefer to live with, your father or your mother?" Again, without a breath in between I responded, "*I told you*, in a tent on the football field." The counselor pressed—that not being an option. I chose neither parent. My mother wept. I asked if I could leave and return to class, and the counselor permitted it.

As I walked down the hall, I felt like I had been ganged up on by adults. I call foul play. The counselor seemed to be sympathetic to my mother, not to be acting on my behalf. I had no desire to speak to the counselor again. I did not need to worry for no effort was expended for a follow up visit. I believe if a student told me they would prefer to live in a tent on the football field than live with either parent, after the student had been referred by a no-nonsense teacher, it may warrant further contact.

After a few weeks of Selma and I staying at friends we had grown weary trying to sneak over to Ventura to get some clothes, shoes or personal items before our mom arrived. I believe the Gaines' were relieved when I told them I was going home and thanked them for allowing me to stay. No questions were asked, like if my father knew. I had not spoken to my dad since he dropped me off at their house. If he was working on a plan, he had not updated me on the progress. My mother did not resist Selma and my homesteading in our room.

It had been about a week or a little more since our return when there was a knock on the door. My sister and I had only been home from school for just a few minutes. Selma was starting down the hall and I was still in the living room pulling off the straps of my book bag. I was closest to the door, so I reached over and turned the knob, opening the door. I let my book bag slide to the floor when I noticed a police deputy with a gun strapped to his side and a paper in his hands standing on the porch. I did not even hear who he asked for and I yelled for mom. Selma echoed my yell for mom. Mom, reacting to the urgency in our voices rushed in from the kitchen to address the deputy.

He shifted his weight as he talked then handed the paper to Mom. I certainly did not understand what he had said. My first thought was he had the wrong house. Mom closed the door. Selma and I both asked her, "What is it? Why did the police come to our door? Why don't you tell us anything?" Mom began to cry and said we were being evicted. "Evicted, what is that?" Mom's response was, "Your dad has stopped paying the rent so now we are being told to leave. We have to be out in thirty days." Panic set in. I felt a sickening, overwhelming nausea, tingling at my fingertips, sit down because you may fall, feeling. The sight of a big, armed, uniformed man at your door telling your family to, "Get Out." It was embarrassing, for I had never seen the police at anyone's doorway. Mom untypically, tried to be calming and said we could find another place to live. How reassuring, as she started to cry again. Selma and I were in our beds while she was on the phone calling people, telling them the story of the latest news and crying, saying she did not know what or how she could do anything. I tried to drown out the sound by folding my head between my pillows. I wanted to scream. I wanted to climb out the window and run, but now knew there was nowhere to go. I clenched my teeth so no sound would fall out of my mouth.

The only way to get through the night was to do the trick I had taught myself over the past weeks. It was to turn any feelings I did not like or would cause me to cry, off, like turning off a water hose outside. You know, so the water would stop flowing out the end. You just turn the handle attached to the house and the water stops running. I then would just become non-feeling, no tears, no laughing, nothing. It usually took a couple of minutes to hear if someone was talking to me but otherwise, I could go on doing what I needed to do. This night what I had to do was sleep.

Another few days had past and mom came in the house in hysterics. She had lost a house located near the high school by twenty minutes. Someone that had seen it right before she was scheduled to view it had put down a deposit. Revealing she had been looking and could not find anything to rent that she could afford in the school district, the tears, sobbing and blaming dad for putting her in this situation rant had begun. A few hours later, it evolved into a drunken rant having Selma and I to use the window escape once again.

It was not too many days into our thirty-day countdown when dad called. I had answered the phone and he wanted to speak to me. It was a *first*, as in never happened before—ever. He went on to ask how we were doing. I informed him of the scary episode that Selma, mom, and I experienced a few days prior with the deputy coming over to tell us to get out of the house and how mom was having a difficult time finding place. He interrupted to say that was the reason he was calling. He said he had an option and he wanted me to talk it over with Sis. He inquired if we would like to move to North Carolina with him. Dad said he would leave it up to what Selma and I decided. He would call back the next day at the same time. He knew mom would not be home at that time.

Now, keeping in mind we had been evicted, soon to be tossed out. It is possible the eviction could have been encouraged by my father. Our mother is a drunk and experiencing great difficulty finding a place in our school district. If she did find somewhere to live, the window escape access in the bedroom Selma and I share needs to be a top priority. The decision to leave our schools and friends is left up to us (I was thirteen years old and Selma twelve years old).

Selma had heard part of the conversation with dad, and I filled in the blanks. We deduced the choice was simple: to stay where we had nowhere to live or move where there would be a place to live. I did not want to leave my school, my boyfriend, and friends yet the last several months had proved to Sis and me it is important to have somewhere to live. North Carolina was a place where dad's family resided. The family loved us and if the need presented, we may not have to stand with hat in our hand and plead to have a roof over our head.

How could she and I do anything about this situation? We were not able to go get a job to pay rent, utilities or even pay for school lunch. There was really no choice. Selma and I had to move if we were going to have a place to stay out of the rain and food to eat. Why was this a choice? Dad called the next day at the appointed time, and I gave him our "Choice."

I had been able to talk to Wayne almost nightly since moving back to Ventura. He offered hope and I doubt he would ever know how much those chats helped me. if nothing else, I was able to rest from being on high alert every minute. My heart rate was normal. My jaw was not clenched so I did not have a headache.

There for a short period of time I could relax, laugh, smile, and just be a girl. It was difficult to tell him about the move to North Carolina. I did not know when it would happen so there was no specifics given. The next week at school I started to push him away by starting an argument over something meaningless. The understanding of what I was doing may not have been realized at the time. It was shortly thereafter.

***

Leaving the Woods

You get a strange feeling when you're about to leave a place
Like you'll not only miss the people you love
But you'll miss the person YOU are now at this time and place
Because YOU will never be this person again

—Azar Nafasi

Days later, another call came from dad to inform us that he would be there to pick us up from school on the next day to go to North Carolina. I had hoped this call would not come. Selma knew of the arrangements when I hung up the phone.

She knew I was having a harder time leaving. She made friends anywhere and everywhere. There was a sinking feeling setting on me—a heaviness from my shoulders down. I placed my back against the hallway wall and slid to the floor, closing my eyes tightly to not see what was disappearing.

The morning arrived much too quickly. Breakfast was far from being on my priority list, so I skipped it. I told Mom bye and headed out for the bus like usual. Things were different though. I knew that I would not walk to the bus from Ventura Drive in Wando Woods again. I tried not to be the whole picture viewer, but I could not help it. No difference the way I viewed it, from a few steps back or a telescope from Venus, the deep hurt would not vary.

The ultimate challenge was to get through this without crying. I did not know what time my dad was coming to whisk me away. I went through each class period holding my breath trying to remember some of my favorite people's faces. My brain was too distracted to freeze frame anyone unless they were already imprinted in my brain waves.

Lunch time was due soon. I dreaded the upcoming dance of hiding from one area to another. I had not spoken to Wayne to tell him I was leaving. I did tell a friend to let him know today was the day and a few sentimental things. The bell rang and with my startle reflex in high gear, I jumped like a wild animal had just snarled its teeth at me.

How nice it would be if I could go find Levi guy and stretch out my hand, waiting for his to hold unto mine. I was not fond of the lunchroom and anyone that knew me was very aware of that fact. The best place to hide out for the day was, the stinking lunchroom. I went in and parked at an empty table. The tables were becoming crowded and people I knew were coming in. I exited, walking out toward the smoking porch where students were permitted to smoke cigarettes. No, I was not a smoker, therefore that area was another place to hide for a few.

Finally, the first bell rang ending my lunch time. I walked slowly, to allow Wayne the opportunity to head on to class before I crossed the threshold of the annex building for the last time. I caught a glimpse of him opening the door to the second floor to take the stairs. My breath caught. I shook the thoughts out of my head and moved on to class with Mrs. Gadsen for the last time.

Only minutes in Earth Science, the loudspeaker sputtered, cutting in asking, "Mrs. Gadsen, is Wanda Lefler in your class?" Mrs Gadsen cleared her throat before she responded, "Yes, she is." The voice said, "Please send her to the office to check out." Gathering my belongings, leaving the textbook on the desk I stood up. The class was as quiet as could be, even Mrs. Gadsen had stopped her lesson. She was standing in front of her desk as she always did when teaching. Her chin had tightened to form a dimple. She nodded her head as I crossed in front of her to leave. Greg had pulled on my sleeve as I moved past him. Once I crossed over the doorway, I heard Mrs. Gadsen say, "All right, class. Let us return to our lesson."

Walking to the office past rows of lockers I thought about the first time I entered the hallway and was wowed at how wide the hallways were compared to the elementary school. Pulling the heavy doorway to the office I remembered wondering if there was a strength test for physical education with this door before you are allowed to graduate. There stood my dad half smiling. He had signed me out. *Signed me out.* We, at least he, was ready to go. He stretched out his arm pointing toward the heavy door. Luckily, he opened it, pushing it into the hallway. The front doors were open with sunlight streaking across the door mats inside the doorways. Very much like the sunlight bursting through the water at the pool when swimming up from the deep end—toward the noise and chaos.

I was surprised to see that dad had purchased a yellow Ford Ranchero. It was sitting at the curb, all packed up with my sister sitting in the front seat. She threw her hand up with a half unhappy look on her face. Dad asked if I wanted to squeeze in or ride in the back. Sis scooted over to the middle of the bench seat. There were a few items in the back. I could see my dependable white, Lady Baltimore suitcase set beside my sister's. I climbed in, tossing my book bag in first. I placed my back against the cab facing the school, settling my deflated book bag under my legs. Those moments were better for me to face myself. The advice is to not look back when you are leaving a place. Those words would not have been much help on that day because I was facing what I was leaving while being seated in the back of the truck bed.

My body was unhappy. My head, my heart and way deep down in the core of what was left of me felt too heavy to move. My cheekbones were stinging. I was unable to swallow. I was holding my breath so I would not feel like I had landed hard from a long fall. My tears were hot and dripping slowly one at a time. My teeth were clenched so no sobs could be heard. I had not learned any method to turn off the severe pain.

Today – Moving Forward

I wonder why it is I must wander from place to place like a hummingbird zipping about the flowers. Is it as my husband jests, that I am looking for loose change or more likely, looking for answers?

I seek, a key to open a door to the place I belong. A place where I may be settled in mind and body. A restful place to unpack my suitcase and call home.

The answer for me is, keep your suitcase near and ready, preferably one with wheels. Home may have to be a feeling experienced here and there, every now and then instead of a roof over four walls.

***

LOVE LETTER FROM BOBBY TO INGA

DATED: FRIDAY 4 JUNE 1965

Dear Inga,

Just fine except missing you and the kids. Hope they are fine. It is hot here not like good old N.C. Hope you got your driving licenses.

Well the rocket didn't need the Nimble *(Ship he served on)*. Glad they didn't have any trouble. I mailed you, Roger the rent. I will call when we get back to Charleston. Should be some time Tuesday. I am sending this money. Take care of it. I know you need some.

Tell everyone hello for me and kiss the girls. I love you and miss you darling.

Hope to see you soon.

Love always

Your husband Bob

CPSIA information can be obtained
at www.ICGtesting.com
Printed in the USA
LVHW081503050522
717810LV00062B/1176